For my siblings: Linda, Billy, Laura and Jeanie—
Each influenced this book in their own unique
way and continue to honor our mother's legacy
with every fold of a dumpling, drizzle of sesame
oil and chop of their cleavers.

Katie Chin's
Everyday Chinese Cookbook

101 Delicious Recipes from My Mother's Kitchen

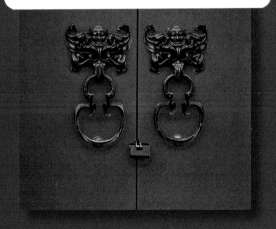

KATIE CHIN

Foreword by Raghavan Iyer

Photography by Masano Kawana

TUTTLE Publishing

Tokyo | Rutland, Vermont | Singapore

Contents

Foreword

Leeann Chin was an extraordinary woman, and in the case of her daughter Katie, the apple certainly didn't fall far from the tree. In the early nineties in Minneapolis, shortly after I had started teaching Indian cuisine at a local cooking school, I had the opportunity to attend a class on Chinese appetizers taught by a well-known restaurateur, Leeann Chin. I arrived early, so I was able to witness her efficient moves as she got a bamboo steamer basket ready on one burner and monitored the temperature of a pot of oil on another, all while simultaneously peeling and deveining shrimp for her cilantro-smothered shrimp dumplings. Assistants hovered around to help, but she was clearly in charge. Her passion for teaching came through during the next few hours, as she showed us how to pleat dumpling wrappers just so—her years of work as a seamstress clearly visible in the perfectly pleated pan-fried dumplings she produced. When one came to rest on my plate, it didn't matter that I was a vegetarian. I inhaled the addictive succulence of that shrimp dumpling in one smooth mouthful.

I remember asking Leeann about the regional Chinese cooking that was reflective of her youthful days, and whether she missed it. "Yes," she replied, looking up at me—but then she explained how she relived those days each time she taught Chinese cooking or made a meal for her family. Those meals, by the way, were nothing like the Chinese-American staples that had become synonymous with her battalion of restaurants. Her business acumen shone through as she admitted to serving Minnesotans foods that she knew would appeal to their palates. "Just a bit sweeter than I eat at home," she clarified.

Years later, I was working with two master chefs from northern China who came to town to do a series of seminars on the noodle-pulling techniques for which they were well known. I took them to Leeann's restaurant, where she was the perfect hostess. The chefs ate the same luncheon buffet that she had single-handedly introduced to hundreds of thousands over the years—nothing "special," nothing different. Out of curiosity, I asked her why. She said they needed to see what was possible in America, and she wanted them to experience what a successful restaurant did to showcase the flavors of a cuisine that was thousands of years old. Leeann was unquestionably a pioneer, and I was fortunate to host an Emmy-winning documentary, *Asian Flavors*, which featured her life and influences in Chinese cooking over the years.

Fast-forward to several years later, when I had the opportunity to connect with Katie Chin. I fell in love with her—with her work, her business acumen, her teaching style—and no wonder: I know how proud she made Leeann. Katie's books are works of passion that showcase her style in terms of accessibility and ease. Paging through this manuscript, I was touched by her poignant stories, laughed out loud when I read about Leeann's candor, and marveled at their mutual passion for sharing the varied cuisine of China. I hope you not only cook from this book, but also curl up with it at night to enjoy the stories that Katie Chin so eloquently weaves throughout her easy recipes.

Raghavan Iyer
author of *660 Curries* and *Indian Cooking Unfolded*

The Wisdom of My Mother's Kitchen

My late mother Leeann and I on the set of our PBS cooking series, *Double Happiness*.

My mother, Leeann Chin, was born in Guangzhou, China, in 1933. She demonstrated a keen knack for numbers, mastering the abacus at the tender age of twelve. She'd draw crowds to her father's grocery store, where onlookers would admire her quick fingers manipulating the beads of the abacus. A tomboy, she soon was delivering fifty-pound bags of rice on the back of her bike, riding up to ninety miles a day.

As a child, my mother was curious about food and cooking, but her mother didn't want her to learn how to cook—that was a job for the hired help. My mother would sneak into the kitchen and follow the family cook around with wide-eyed fascination. She'd watch as the cook's cleaver danced across the wooden chopping block, gracefully mincing garlic; she enjoyed the sight of smoking ginger-infused peanut oil with green onion threads being poured over a freshly steamed sea bass, and the sizzling sound the oil made as it hit the fish.

At the age of seventeen, she escaped the Cultural Revolution and moved to Hong Kong, where a matchmaker paired her with my father, Tony. My parents and my paternal grandmother lived in a modest apartment where my mother adjusted to the bustling streets and bright lights of the city. Although she had followed the family cook around, she had little experience actually cooking on her own; however, she was expected to prepare my father's favorite dishes immediately upon becoming his bride. She started experimenting with the succulent seafood and plump ducks that Hong Kong had to offer, and her love affair with cooking began.

In 1956, my parents and grandmother were given the opportunity to immigrate to Minneapolis, Minnesota, where my aunt "Goo Ma" and uncle "Bue Jang" operated the Kwong Tong Noodle Company. It was a culture and climate shock. My mother did her best to cook her favorite Cantonese dishes, but it was difficult for her to even find fresh ginger at the grocery store. She learned to improvise, and started growing bok choy, Chinese long beans and Asian eggplant in our tiny garden.

In addition to my two sisters who immigrated with my parents from Hong Kong, my mother gave birth to my brother and my other sisters in the mid-1950s through the mid-'60s. Knowing it was hard for her children to assimilate as Chinese-Americans, my mother did everything she could to help us fit in, like bringing us to Sons of Norway events, but every night she made us Chinese food. We didn't fully appreciate the gourmet Chinese meals we were served, and secretly wished we were eating Hamburger Helper like all the other kids. Foolish, I know.

Me as a spiky-haired baby with my family.

My mom with Hillary Clinton.

My mom with her "bestie," Martin Yan.

My mom teaching Chinese cooking classes in the 1970s.

My mother had a talent for sewing (which explains her expert dumpling pleating), and became a seamstress, making fifty cents an hour. A few years on, my mother threw a thank-you luncheon for her sewing clients, thoughtfully crafting a menu of crispy Cantonese egg rolls, silky egg-drop soup, lemon chicken and three-flavor lo mein with homemade egg noodles. As always when she was cooking, she put her affection and gratitude into the food she made. Her customers had never tasted anything like it in their lives, and they encouraged her to start teaching classes and catering.

In those early days, my mother couldn't drive a car, much less afford one, so she had to take the bus to her cooking classes. She couldn't carry everything at once, so she'd leave some of the groceries at the bus stop, get to her destination and turn around and take another bus back to pick up the remaining groceries. And she did this in the wintertime, too! No wonder she gave us that puzzled look whenever any of us complained about anything.

By the mid-1970s, our basement had become a bustling catering kitchen producing tray after tray of *shu mai*, crab wontons, sesame noodles and sweet-and-sour pork. In the Chinese-American tradition of child labor, we'd come home from school, put down our backpacks and start frying. While other kids were ice skating or hanging out at the mall, we were usually making wontons or stringing snow peas, but we didn't mind. We sensed that our mother was serving a greater purpose, and we felt like we were assisting a master performing magic in our kitchen.

One day, she had the opportunity to cater a party attended by Sean Connery and Robert Redford—famous movie stars! We all knew something special was happening to our mother. Soon after, she was given a chance to open her first restaurant. The deal was clinched once investors, including Sean Connery (he was hooked after tasting her food), came on board, and the restaurant was an immediate success. She had introduced authentic Chinese cooking to Minnesotans and they couldn't get enough. Before long, more restaurants followed.

Although she sold the chain to General Mills at one point, she ended up buying it back a few years later. While building her empire, she was full of surprises at every turn. My sister Laura, who worked for the company, told me how my mother would make a calculation in her head and come out with it before the bankers could pull out their calculators; once they checked, they'd say, "Wow, she's right."

At the height of her career, when she was running more than thirty restaurants, she remained focused on the quality of the food. I remember one of her managers telling me about the time she came in after a board meeting during the lunch rush. She saw the kitchen was overwhelmed, so she rolled up the sleeves of her Chanel bouclé jacket and started stir-frying. As much as she was a mother to us, she had over a thousand employees who also considered her to be their mother, with her strict, yet nurturing, style of training and management.

My mom with Robert Redford at her restaurant in Minnetonka, Minnesota.

My mom at one of her restaurants helming the stir-fry line.

My mom, me and my sister Jeannie preparing for Chinese New Year celebration.

The basic stir-fry technique demonstrated on page 18.

My mother left the company in the late 1990s, but the Leeann Chin restaurant chain is still alive and well, with over forty-five locations spread across the Twin Cities area.

This is where I come in.

About fifteen years ago, I was in living in Los Angeles working as a film and television marketing executive, and I had completely forgotten how to cook (I could still make 5,000 pieces of shrimp toast, no problem, but a dinner party was something else entirely). My favorite thing to make for dinner was reservations. I was so busy trying to make my mother proud by succeeding in my marketing career that I had actually done the opposite by forgetting how to cook.

I invited some clients over for dinner, and had a panic attack because I didn't know what I was doing. I called my mother for advice, and instead of telling me what to do she jumped on a plane with a box of frozen lemon chicken on dry ice. Once she arrived on my doorstep, she not only cooked the entire dinner, but kept everyone believing that I had cooked the whole thing by myself. That's just the kind of mom she was. But when she opened my refrigerator to find only champagne and yogurt, she was mortified, and set out to teach me how to cook again.

Through a series of dinner parties for my friends, my passion for Asian cooking was reignited. People told me, "You really make Chinese cooking look easy, like I could do it myself." Feeling inspired and glad to be back in touch with my culinary roots, I quit my job, and my mother and I co-authored a Chinese cookbook together. From there, we

started a Pan-Asian catering business called Double Happiness Catering.

In between our catering gigs, we were lucky enough to travel to China together to co-host a Food Network special called *My Country, My Kitchen*, as well as to New York for numerous appearances together on the *Today* show. The next natural step was to do a cooking show: we co-hosted the national PBS cooking series *Double Happiness*, a mother-daughter Chinese cooking show shot in Hawaii.

My mother was the toughest boss I've ever had (and believe me, I had some tough ones working in Hollywood all those years). She set the same standards for me as she did for herself, and I never felt like I was living up to her expectations. She would reprimand me, "Your egg rolls are not wrapped firmly enough"; "You should make double the pleats on that *shu mai*." One time, on our cooking show, I said, "If you don't have Asian hot sauce, you can use Mexican hot sauce instead. Right, mom?" Her deadpan response on camera was, "No." I recognize now that she just wanted me to be the best I could be.

With my mother as commander-in-chief, and me as her willing apprentice, our catering business took off and we were soon doing star-studded parties and high-fashion events. She realized I would never learn to handle the cooking alone if she was always there to lead me, so she announced one day out of the blue that she was going to Europe for three months with a friend. I was left to my own devices and a deep fryer and was forced to figure things out on

On location in Guangzhou, China filming our Food Network special, *My Country, My Kitchen.*

To make Hoisin Lacquered Ribs like these, see page 89.

Picking out prawns in Guangzhou, China.

My twins Dylan and Becca having a ball making dumpling filling.

my own. That summer, I finally sprouted my culinary wings and flew from her bird's nest soup.

I retired from catering when I became pregnant with our own Double Happiness, twins Dylan and Becca, and focused my energy on my blog and cookbooks. Although she only knew them as toddlers, my mother left an indelible mark on my twins. To this day, their favorite foods are dumplings and noodles; instead of baking cookies, they'd rather be folding potstickers.

My mother passed away in 2010. She spent the last few years of her life visiting her son, her daughters and her grandchildren. She cooked her way across the country, filling our freezers with stir-fries and soups. To the end, food was the focus of my mother's life. My sister Jeannie told me about my mom being taken away by an ambulance a few months before her passing. As they were lifting her into the ambulance, she called out to my sister, "Don't forget to eat the spicy ground pork noodles I left in the fridge!"

Out of our amazing culinary journey, I treasure the times we spent alone together in the kitchen the most. In those quiet moments, rolling out dough for dumplings or gently simmering sauces for a whole fish, she'd open up and tell me about her life. She revealed sometimes difficult memories, from her childhood in China to assimilating as an immigrant to the challenges of being a wife and a mother, as well as a minority businesswoman—all things she didn't want to burden us with as children. I realized she used cooking as an escape from her many struggles, and that's where she found

joy. Cooking was a kind of alchemy for her. This, and so much more about life, I learned in the kitchen from my mother.

I hope you enjoy this collection of Chin family recipes. Some are taken from my mother's personal vault, like the time-honored classics she learned how to make in China, while others reflect our Chinese-American childhood. I've also included recipes that my mother and I developed together for our catering business, as well as some that I've developed more recently, inspired by her teachings. I've also woven personal recollections and anecdotes throughout this book. I wanted to share the inspiration behind some of the recipes, as well as fun memories from our childhood and later years of cooking and eating with our mother.

My pioneering mother instilled a passion for Chinese cooking in me, and I am so honored to carry on her legacy. She was revered for her ability to demystify Chinese cooking and simplify it for the everyday home cook. Carrying her torch, I hope I can show you how easy Chinese cooking can truly be. If I can do it, you can do it.

Thank you for keeping her memory alive by making the recipes in this book. I hope they bring some wisdom to your kitchen, joy to your taste buds and gratification to your bellies.

Happy cooking!

Katie Chin

Katie Chin
author of *Everyday Thai Cooking*

Understanding Chinese Ingredients

When my mother Leeann immigrated to Minnesota in 1956, she couldn't find bok choy or oyster sauce, let alone fresh ginger, at the grocery store. She improvised and still managed to make incredibly delicious Chinese dishes for us (I am still baffled by this and her other magician-like powers in the kitchen). Today, much has changed: it's not uncommon to find black bean sauce, Asian eggplant and cellophane noodles at the regular grocery store, or daikon radish and Chinese long beans at your local farmer's market. The majority of the ingredients needed for the recipes in this book can be found at your neighborhood market, with some recipes requiring an occasional trip to an Asian store or some on-line shopping. In this section, I've compiled the key ingredients used in Chinese cooking. Over time, you'll discover the ingredients you'll want to keep on hand to make your favorite Chinese dishes.

Baby Corn These miniature ears of corn are often used in stir-fries. Harvesting the grain early, while the ears are immature, allows for the whole cob to be consumed. Baby corn comes canned and ready to cook. Best known for its cameo in the movie *Big*, it adds a unique texture to any stir-fry dish.

Bamboo Shoots There are the part of the bamboo plant that is harvested before it matures. Available fresh, canned or bottled, bamboo shoots are found in Asian markets and many grocery stores. Any unused bamboo shoots should be stored in water and kept in the refrigerator. Change water daily to preserve freshness.

Black Beans, Fermented These fermented, salted black soybeans have a distinctive pungent aroma, and add a very rich flavor when combined with garlic, ginger and other flavors. They come packed in plastic bags, or are made into a sauce and sold in a jar. If purchased in plastic bags, they should be rinsed in warm water before using to remove excess salt, and refrigerated after opening.

Black Mushrooms, Dried These are incredibly versatile, adding an amazingly rich flavor to stir-fries, soups and noodle dishes. They must be presoaked in warm water before using. When soaked, they plump up and have a delicious meaty taste and texture. If you can't find dried black mushrooms, dried shiitake mushrooms can be substituted.

Bok Choy A crisp vegetable shaped rather like a celery plant, bok choy has whitish stalks and deep-green leaves. The smaller the head of bok choy, the more tender it will be. Baby bok choy, the smallest kind, is the most expensive. Bok choy is available in most supermarkets. Shanghai Bok Choy, which can be found in many Asian markets, is dark green in color and slightly bitter, and is highly prized. Bok choy is very nutrient-dense—so you can enjoy this tasty vegetable and load up on folic acid and vitamins A and C while you're at it.

Brown Bean Paste It is the ground version of brown beans used in sauces; it is used throughout northern China. A thick, salty and rich cousin of black bean sauce, it can be purchased in a jar and stored indefinitely. A little of this savory paste goes a long way, so use it sparingly. You can find brown bean paste at Asian markets and online resources.

Chilies, Dried Red These dried red peppers are usually

very hot. They are an essential ingredient in many Sichuan dishes, and can be used to season oil. Used whole, they impart a lovely chili flavor without the heat. Chiles de árbol can be substituted if you can't find dried Chinese chilies.

Chili Garlic Sauce It is the perfect combination of zesty chilies and fragrant garlic. It's very versatile, and can be used for marinating, as a dipping sauce and for whenever you want to add a kick in the pants to a stir-fry dish. I prefer the Lee Kum Kee brand. Sambal Oelek is an acceptable substitute.

Chili Paste Also known as chili bean sauce, is made from crushed fresh red chilies, soybeans, salt and garlic. It varies from being hot to very hot. Sold in jars, it is rich, spicy and earthy; it is used both as a condiment and as a seasoning for sauces and stir-fries.

Chinese Black Vinegar Often labeled as "Chinkiang vinegar," is made from fermented rice, wheat, barley or sorghum. It is a tart and smoky dark vinegar that is used as a dipping sauce and in cooking.

Chinese Broccoli (Gailan/Kalian) This leafy vegetable, also known as Chinese kale, has thick, flat glossy leaves and thick stems. Sweet and slightly bitter, Chinese Broccoli is a versatile vegetable that's a great addition to many stir-fry dishes and a delicious side dish drizzled with oyster sauce. Chinese broccoli is a nutrient-dense food, and is an excellent source of folic acid, vitamin A, vitamin C and vitamin K.

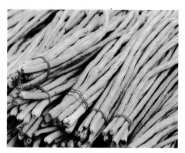

Chinese Long Beans Also known as yard-long beans, Chinese long beans really can grow that long! To be used as a vegetable, though, the bean pods are picked before they reach maturity. Chinese long beans can be found coiled or tied into bunches at Asian markets and some grocery stores. They are typically blanched and then stir-fried.

Chinese Chives Also known as garlic chives, are earthy yet delicate. They are similar to Western chives, but are wider and more pungent. The less-common Chinese yellow chives are more delicate in flavor and taste more like an onion than a chive. The yellow variety is grown in the dark and deprived of sunlight, so the leaves are stripped of their green color.

Cloud Ears Also known as Chinese tree fungus, cloud ears come dried and should be soaked in warm water for 20 minutes before using; any hard portions should be trimmed and discarded. After soaking, they swell up to look like little clouds. Cloud ears have a mild smoky flavor.

Fish Sauce Though it's best known as an ingredient in Southeast Asian cooking, fish sauce is not uncommon in Chinese cuisine. It is called "fish mist" in China, and is used by the Chiu Chow people in southern China. Made from fermented anchovies, fish sauce has a distinct fishy, briny aroma that dissipates upon cooking, lending a unique salty flavor to dishes.

Five-Spice Powder As the name suggests, this is a combination of five ground spices: star anise, Sichuan pepper, fennel, cloves and cinnamon. Pungent, complex and spicy with a hint of sweetness, five-spice powder can be found in Asian markets and some grocery stores.

Noodles Chinese cooking uses many types of noodles, from egg noodles and rice stick noodles to flat rice noodles and bean-thread noodles.

Egg Noodles are so versatile; they can be bought dried and kept on hand for a chow mein dish or a quick Chinese noodle soup. My mother's homemade egg noodles were the best—her recipe, made with only eggs and flour, is on page 140. **Rice Stick Noodles**, a.k.a. rice vermicelli, are skinny dried noodles made from rice flour and water. Rice sticks can be used in soups and salads. To prepare, place rice sticks in a large bowl. Add hot water to cover. Let stand until softened, about 10 minutes. Drain and rinse with cool water. When deep-fried, they puff up to ten times their size! **Flat Rice Noodles** can be bought dried or fresh. They are also made of rice flour and water, and are thick and chewy—they're the signature noodle used in Chow Fun dishes. Fresh flat rice noodles are white, with a shiny oil coating. When buying fresh flat rice noodles for the recipes in this book, make sure they're pre-cut. **Bean-Thread Noodles**, a.k.a. cellophane noodles, are made from mung beans that have been mashed and strained, then formed into very thin white noodles. Bean-thread noodles need to be soaked in hot water for 10 minutes before using; they will turn clear with cellophane-like appearance. They are gluten-free.

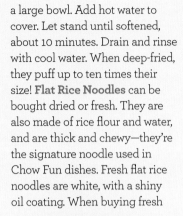
Egg Noodles

Flat Rice Noodles

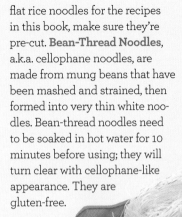
Bean-Thread Noodles

Hoisin Sauce Hoisin sauce is traditionally made from red rice brewed with soybean paste, garlic, sugar, star anise, chili paste and other spices. It ranges in color from reddish brown to mahogany. It is an excellent marinade, glaze and dipping sauce. It has a very strong taste that can overpower other ingredients, however, so it should be added a little at a time until the desired flavor and heat is reached. Hoisin sauce is widely available at grocery stores and Asian markets. You can also make it from scratch; see the recipe on page 25.

Lotus Root This oblong beige vegetable is actually the root of the lotus flower. It contains a surprising system of baffles and chambers that, when the root is sliced, make a charming pattern of holes. Lotus root adds crunch in salads, soups and braised dishes; it can also be eaten raw or briefly stir-fried. It should be peeled and sliced before using. Lotus root can be bought at Asian grocery stores.

Lychees Mildly sweet in flavor with a floral smell, lychees are available fresh or canned. Fresh lychees, which consist of a berry-like fruit encased in a brown and pink shell, are becoming more common in Asian markets. The canned variety is widely available.

Plum Sauce At once both sweet and sour, plum sauce is used as a dipping sauce for spring rolls and other deep-fried dishes, as well as on barbecued meats. It is made from plums, sugar, vinegar, salt, ginger and chili peppers.

Chinese Rice Wine It lends an unmistakable flavor and fragrance to a variety of Chinese dishes, from dumplings and stir-fries to clay-pot dishes and marinades. Fragrant, amber-colored and slightly nutty, Chinese rice wine (also called Shaoxing wine) is made from fermented rice and yeast. It's a staple in my pantry, and I find it indispensable. If you can't find Chinese rice wine, then dry cooking sherry is fine as a substitute.

Sichuan Peppercorns These tiny crimson pods, integral to many Sichuan dishes, create a unique tingling sensation in the mouth. More lemony and exotic than spicy, Sichuan peppercorns are paired with chilies to achieve *mala* flavor, a key characteristic of Sichuan cooking.

Sesame Oil, Toasted or Dark Toasted sesame oil is made from toasted sesame seeds. It is used as a seasoning to enhance many Chinese dishes with its signature nutty sesame flavor. Only a few drops are needed to season a dish or enhance a marinade. Sesame oil can turn rancid pretty quickly, so it should be stored away from heat and light.

Soy Sauce It comes in three grades: light, medium and dark. Lighter kinds of soy sauce are commonly used for dipping, while dark soy sauce, also known as black soy sauce, tends to be used in cooking. Dark soy sauce is aged longer, making it slightly sweeter and thicker. Molasses or caramel may be added to deepen its color and thicken its consistency. Heating dark soy sauce releases its full, rich flavor in sauces and gravies; it is also used in stir-fries and noodle dishes.

Wrappers Chinese people love to wrap their food! From wontons to dumplings, everything tastes better wrapped up and steamed or fried. Most Chinese-style wrappers are made from flour and water, and are differentiated mainly by their shape, thickness and size. I like to keep all types of wrappers on hand in my freezer because they're so versatile and handy for last-minute entertaining.

Wonton Wrappers are thin and square. Many people use them to make ravioli (who knew?). **Potsticker Wrappers** (a.k.a. Dumpling Wrappers or Gyoza Wrappers) are similar to wonton wrappers, but are round. When making potstickers or other dumplings, you can cut wonton wrappers into a round shape with a cookie cutter. **Egg Roll Wrappers** are like wonton wrappers, but larger.

They come in 9-in (23-cm) squares. **Spring Roll Wrappers** are used to make spring rolls, which have a crispier, more delicate texture than egg rolls. They are white and don't contain eggs. They are usually sold in the freezer section at Asian markets. Before using, you should separate the sheets by pulling them apart once they've thawed. Spring roll wrappers are used for

other appetizers, too, like Firecracker Shrimp (page 43). **Rice Paper Wrappers** are made from a dough of rice flour and water, which is spread into thin sheets and sun dried. They must be briefly dipped in warm water before using. They're used for roll-ups, like chilled spring rolls.

Wonton Wrappers

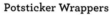

Potsticker Wrappers

Rice Paper Wrappers

Star Anise It is the seedpod of a small tree found throughout Asia. The star-shaped spice has a warm, rich and pungent aroma of licorice, cinnamon and clove. The actual seeds inside the pod are tiny and black, and have no flavor. Used whole, star anise adds a subtle aroma; or it may be ground for maximum flavor. It is a popular ingredient in soups, curries, sweets and teas. A substitute for star anise is a blend of ground cloves and cinnamon.

Straw Mushrooms These are so named because they are cultivated on beds of straw. They are actually shaped like little helmets, and have a delicate, sweet flavor. They are the most widely used mushroom in traditional Chinese cooking, and are added to soups, curries, stir-fries, and more. Fresh straw mushrooms can be hard to find in the United States, but the canned variety should be available at most Asian markets.

Water Chestnuts These are a vegetable that grows in Asian marshes. They have a delicate flavor, and add a nice crunchy texture to stir-fries and soups. Water chestnuts are available canned or fresh. An interesting alternative to water chestnuts is peeled jicama root.

Basic Cooking Techniques and Tips

Many people's attitude toward Chinese cooking is the same as their relationship status on Facebook: "It's complicated." A lot of people are intimidated by Chinese cooking because it seems so involved. The truth is, if you have the right tools on hand and learn the basic time-honored Chinese cooking techniques (which are used over and over again in this book), it isn't complicated at all. In fact, you can make most of these recipes with the pots and pans you have in your kitchen right now. I actually just taught a Chinese cooking class for six twelve-year-old boys, and they couldn't believe how easy it was to make Chinese food (I heard a lot of "Oh, so that's how you do it... cool!"). They practically jumped for joy when they got to make their own dumplings. One mother was astounded when her son ate a dumpling filled with tofu and veggies; she called later that day to report that he had made the recipe again for his whole family! No matter whether you're steaming, deep-frying or stir-frying, you'll be able to master everything from Orange Chicken to Steamed Cantonese Whole Fish in no time if you use this section as your guide.

Seasoning a Wok

I've been asked if seasoning a wok involves spices! In actuality, seasoning a wok is a process that makes it rust-resistant while creating a natural nonstick finish at the same time. It also improves the flavor of stir-fried dishes. Only iron, cast-iron, steel and carbon-steel woks require seasoning, because these are porous materials prone to rust. You don't need to season a nonstick wok.

The process of seasoning creates layers and layers of burnt oil coatings on the surface of the metals, which covers the pores and protects them from rusting or corroding upon exposure to water or acids.

Here's How to Season Your Wok

1 If your wok is new, it will have a thin factory coating that must be removed before the first use. To do this, wash the wok inside and out with a stainless-steel scrubber, dish soap, and hot water. Rinse and dry it over low heat.
2 To begin the seasoning process, place the wok over high heat. Tilt and turn the wok as it heats until it becomes a yellowish-blueish color. Remove from heat.

3 Using a paper towel, wipe the inside of the wok with a small amount of vegetable oil.
4 Turn heat to medium-low. Place wok on burner for 10 minutes.
5 Wipe with a fresh paper towel. There will be black residue on the paper towel. Repeat steps 3 and 4 about three times, adding small amounts of oil, until there is no longer black residue on the paper towel when wiped.
6 Ta-da! You have seasoned your wok and are now ready to stir-fry.

Cleaning Your Seasoned Wok

Now that you've created a beautiful nonstick coating on your wok, you'll want to protect it. Don't use abrasive materials like steel wool when cleaning, and never use soap on your wok. Just run it under hot water and use a soft cleaning brush or sponge to remove food particles. You may need to soak it in hot water for few minutes to remove stubborn bits.

The best way to dry a wok after it's been cleaned is to place it on low heat until all the water evaporates. If you put your wok away before it's completely dry, it will develop rust spots.

Mastering Chinese Stir-Frying

Chinese stir-frying is all about the preparation. Once you have all your stir-fry ingredients cleaned, cut and ready to go, the rest should be easy-peasy and super-duper fast. I mean really, *really* fast. The key to great stir-frying is heating your wok or skillet up very hot so the proteins are nicely seared and the veggies are tender but crisp. You want to keep things moving. The term stir-frying is a bit of a misnomer because the action is more about tossing and flipping than it is about stirring.

It's important to read each recipe carefully so you'll see whether a certain vegetable should be blanched before it gets added to the wok or pan. For blanching, certain vegetables, like broccoli or snow peas, are dropped in boiling water for a minute or two and then placed into an ice-water bath. Blanching preserves the vibrant color of vegetables, cuts down on cooking time and ensures a tender-crisp result. Some vegetables take longer than others, so be sure to read the entire recipe carefully before you begin.

To save time, I often purchase my stir-fry veggies from the salad bar at the local grocery store. Not only is everything is clean and pre-cut, but it also cuts down on waste, especially when you're cooking for one or two, because you only buy what you need.

I like to arrange all of my ingredients on a sheet pan in the order they'll be added to the wok or skillet. This is really helpful, especially when you're making multiple courses. If you're really organized, like my nephew Logan, you can number the ingredients in the order they should be placed in your wok or skillet if you want—toddler flash cards come in handy for this. Also, have all your tools ready to go, arranged in the order you'll be using them.

It's also important to allow the wok or skillet to heat up before adding the oil; you then swirl the pan to coat the surface. The wok or pan is ready when a drop of water sizzles and evaporates right away. Ensure that your skillet has high enough walls so the ingredients don't fly out as you're turning them.

I also like to use a firm spatula, not a flimsy one. A sturdy spatula helps you take control of your stir-frying and allows you to get underneath the ingredients so you can lift them and flip them as they cook. After all, stir-frying is not about stirring; rather, you continuously toss and flip the ingredients so they are all evenly cooked.

Cooking a Perfect Pot of Rice

I'm going to let you in on a little secret: white rice needs to be washed before you steam it. This has been a life-altering discovery for some of my friends. When you wash your rice, you eliminate the excess starch that gets released into the water and reabsorbed during cooking, resulting in mushy rice. Once you get rid of that excess starch you will enjoy the lightest, fluffiest rice ever. (You can thank me later.) In many Chinese

To stir-fry, heat oil in a wok or skillet over moderately high heat and then add aromatics such as garlic, ginger and shallots.

Allow the aromatics to become fragrant, about 30–60 seconds.

Add protein and/or vegetables as directed by the recipe and toss and flip quickly so all of the ingredients are cooked evenly.

families, it's the job of the youngest child to wash the rice. Being the youngest in my family, I'm a bona-fide rice-washing expert!

How to Wash Your Rice

Fill a pot with 1 cup (185 g) raw long-grain white rice and cool water. Swirl the water around with your hands and wash the rice by rubbing it gently between your fingers, then drain. Repeat this process until the water runs clear, usually about 5 or 6 times. After the last rinse, carefully drain all the water from the pot.

Measure Water the Mount Fuji Way

I learned to measure the water for preparing rice with a method used in many Asian households, sometimes called the Mount Fuji technique. With the tip of your index finger just touching the surface of the rice, add water until it reaches your first knuckle. You may feel most comfortable using a measuring cup or going by the lines on the side of your rice-cooker bowl, but know that millions of Asian families swear by this technique. Only use the Mount Fuji technique for preparing white rice—not brown, black or red rice.

How to Cook Your Rice

Add water to the washed rice using the Mount Fuji technique, or add 1 cup (250 ml) water. Bring the rice and water to a boil over high heat. As soon as the water boils, lower the heat to a simmer and cover. Cook at a gentle simmer until the water is completely absorbed and the rice is tender, about 12 minutes. Remove from heat and let sit for 10 minutes with the lid on before serving. One cup (185 g) of raw rice will yield 3 cups (450 g) of cooked rice.

If you're using a rice cooker, wash the rice in the rice-cooker bowl. Use the 1 cup (185 g) raw rice to 1 cup (250 ml) water ratio and cook according to the instruction manual.

How to Deep-Fry

Who doesn't love the first crispy bite of an egg roll or the satisfying crunch of a wonton? Many Chinese appetizers are deep-fried; in entrées like Lemon Chicken or Sesame Scallops, pieces of meat are battered and

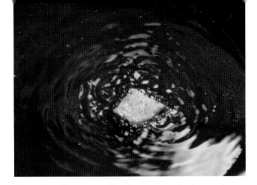

The oil is hot enough when a 1-inch (2.5-cm) cube of white bread floats to the top immediately and browns within 60 seconds.

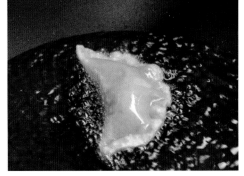

Place the item(s) in the oil. Make sure you don't fry too many pieces at once or the temperature will drop, resulting in sogginess.

Turn the items to brown evenly.

Line a baking sheet with a paper towel in advance so you can remove browned items from the oil promptly to drain and cool.

dropped into a hot oil bath until they achieve the ultimate golden, crunchy goodness.

Many people are scared to deep-fry. They think that oil will inevitably splatter all over the place, and that the food usually turns out soggy. Well, I'm here to debunk those deep-frying myths. First of all, you need to use a pan that's deep enough to eliminate the splatter factor. It's not necessary to use a wok when deep-frying, but you must always use a pan deep enough to adequately cover the item you are frying. For example, if you are using 2 inches (5 cm) of oil, you must leave 6 inches (15 cm) of space above the oil.

Secondly, deep-frying requires very high heat levels (350°F to 375°F / 175°C to 190°C). Use a deep-frying thermometer to monitor the temperature. If you don't have one, you can determine when the oil is ready by dropping a 1-inch (2.5-cm) cube

of white bread into the oil. If it browns in 60 seconds, you're ready to proceed. Make sure the oil isn't too hot, as that will result in food that's overcooked on the outside and undercooked on the inside. If the oil begins to smoke, immediately turn off the heat for a few minutes and let the oil return to 350°F (175°C). Always heat oil uncovered to prevent overheating.

If the temperature is too low, the food will soak up too much oil. Adding too many pieces of food to the oil at once will cause the oil temperature to drop, so just cook a few items at a time. It's also important to dry the food completely before deep-frying, especially before you dip it into batter or marinade.

I recommend using vegetable oil or corn oil for deep-frying. These oils have a high "smoke point," meaning they don't break

down at high temperatures. Oils with a low smoke point, like olive oil, should not be used for deep-frying.

Lastly, always have a paper-towel-lined sheet pan ready to place your items on after they've been fried.

Steaming Successfully

Steaming is the healthiest method in Chinese cooking. When steaming, make sure to bring water to a rolling boil and maintain the heat level while cooking. It's important to ensure there is enough water so it doesn't evaporate and leave you with a scorched pot. If you don't have a steamer, you can use your own stockpot and a heat-safe plate or platter to steam. Simply set two empty cans (such as empty tuna fish cans) in the pot to raise the plate 2 inches above the water. When steaming dumplings, you can place sliced carrots under the dumplings to prevent them from sticking, or set them on parchment paper with holes cut in it. Whether you use a wok, stockpot or traditional steamer, make sure the items are raised above the water and that the lid fits securely.

Eliminating Shrimp's "Fishy" Taste

Ever wonder why the shrimp in Chinese dishes tastes so fresh? Well, my mother taught me a little secret: soak your shrimp in salt water before you cook it. The salt eliminates any fishiness, making shrimp dishes come alive with freshness and letting the shrimp's naturally sweet and delicate flavor shine through.

Brine the Shrimp

For every 1 lb (500 g) of shrimp, place 2 cups (500 ml) water and 1 teaspoon of salt in a bowl. Stir to dissolve. Place the shrimp in the salt water for 5 minutes. Rinse with cold water and drain. Pat dry with a paper towel, and the shrimp are ready to cook!

Basic Tools and Utensils

Wok or Skillet

The wok was invented in China over a thousand years ago. It is central to Chinese cooking and other Asian cuisines because of its unique concave shape and ability to heat up quickly. And let's face it, a billion Chinese people can't be wrong. The wok is incredibly versatile, used for everything from stir-frying and deep-frying to steaming and braising. My mom even fried hamburgers and popped popcorn in her wok when we were little!

The most common types of wok are cast iron and carbon steel. I recommend carbon steel because it heats up quickly and retains heat well. The most user-friendly size is 14 inches (29 cm). Larger woks can become unwieldy. Look for a wok with sturdy handles and a lid. I use both a cast-iron wok and a carbon-steel wok in my kitchen. Some wok purists turn their nose up at nonstick woks, but I say go with whatever works for you. If

you're going to use nonstick, I recommend a premium brand like Calphalon, Circulon or All-Clad. Carbon-steel and cast-iron woks need to be seasoned. See page 18 for instructions on how to season your wok.

A flat-bottomed wok is the best shape for an American stovetop. If you have a powerful range, like Viking or Wolf, then you can get away with a round bottomed wok with a stand, as these stoves produce enough heat to thoroughly heat a round bottom.

I have friends who suffer from wok anxiety. They just don't feel comfortable using one, or the one they have is lost somewhere in the attic. If you can relate, you are not alone. Rest assured that you can make everything in this book in a frying pan or skillet, as modern stoves deliver high enough heat levels to achieve the even distribution required for Chinese cooking. Just make sure you use a skillet with high

enough edges, or else the ingredients will fly out of your pan. When deep-frying, make sure to use a deep skillet (see pages 19–20 for more information). I like to use a nonstick skillet, because less oil is needed and meat won't stick as much. Look for nonstick pans which are PFOA-, lead- and cadmium-free. I prefer ceramic nonstick pans. Just make sure to use a spatula that's safe for nonstick surfaces to avoid scratching the pan.

For deep-frying and steaming, I like to use an electric wok that I can place in a separate area of my kitchen. This provides extra space if I'm also stir-frying or braising a separate dish on my stovetop.

Knives

Chinese food is all about the prep, as everything generally cooks quickly—especially stir-fry dishes. Preparation involves lots of mincing, chopping and dicing, so invest in quality knives and keep them sharp. A standard 8-inch (20-cm) chef's knife should do the trick, along with some good paring knives.

My mother always used a Chinese cleaver, and you may want to consider picking one up in Chinatown or online. Like woks, Chinese cleavers are extremely versatile. You can chop, dice, shred, slice and even hack chicken bones to pieces. Plus, you'll look pretty fierce wielding one! Make sure to purchase a cleaver that fits comfortably in your hand and isn't too heavy for you to handle.

Rice Cooker

If there's one thing you should invest in when it comes to Chinese cooking, it's a rice cooker. Who *doesn't* need a device that can do the thinking for you? A rice cooker has an internal temperature sensor that can sense when all the water has been absorbed by the rice or grains in the pot. It then miraculously switches to a setting that keeps the rice warm, so you don't have to do a thing and you don't have to worry about your rice burning. This is especially great when you're entertaining and trying to juggle a few recipes at once.

There are several models available, ranging in price from $10 to more than $500. The higher-priced models have fuzzy-logic technology, which means they contain a computer chip that can calibrate the temperature and water quantity for a superior end product. I recommend Zojirushi and Cuisinart fuzzy-logic rice cookers.

For the recipes in this book, you can use any type of rice cooker. I have to say that fuzzy-logic models produce perfect fluffy rice every time (although the run-of-the-mill budget-priced rice cooker that I grew up with served our family just fine).

Clay Pot

A clay pot is another versatile tool to have in the Chinese kitchen. You can roast and braise with it and make soups and stews in it. Clay pots are most often used for braising and stewing in Chinese cooking because they retain heat so well.

Clay is a porous material which, when soaked in water and heated in the oven, provides slow evaporation of steam from the pores. This moist cooking environment results in incredibly flavorful and tender meats. It's super healthy, too, because you're not cooking with a lot of oil. Another wonderful thing about a clay pot is that it can go straight from oven to table. Not only is it a terrific cooking vessel, it's a unique and tasteful serving piece. I guarantee at least one "Ahhh" and maybe one "Ooh!" when you set it on the table at your next dinner party. You can find clay pots at Asian markets or online. Clay pots should simply be washed with hot water. The use of soap isn't recommended.

Bamboo Steamers

I stock up on all different sizes of bamboo steamers because I steam so many different things in them, from dumplings to whole fish, and because they're so pretty and fun to use when I entertain. (I guess you could call me a "basket" case.) For everyday cooking, one large bamboo steamer with a lid should be adequate. If you like to entertain, buy a stackable set, which usually comes with three baskets. Make sure your basket fits properly in your wok or pan; the pan should be about 3 inches (7.5 cm) wider than the basket. Always make certain you have enough boiling water in the pan, and be sure that the basket sits about 2 inches (5 cm) above the water. Cover tightly with the lid before steaming.

Strainer or Slotted Spoon

I recommend a traditional Chinese-style strainer with a long bamboo handle (often called a "spider"). I'm not sure why, but this utensil sometimes makes me feel like a superhero, especially when I'm trying to fry egg rolls for a hundred guests. It's made out of wire mesh and is great for removing deep-fried foods from oil as well as removing blanched foods from boiling water. You can find this type of strainer at an Asian market or specialty gourmet store. I find it to be an indispensable tool in my kitchen. You can also use a wide, Western-style slotted spoon in place of a Chinese-style strainer, but don't use it for deep-frying if it's made of plastic.

Wooden Spatula

Steel Spatula

Spatula

Everything moves really fast when you're stir-frying, and you need a proper spatula for even cooking. As mentioned previously, stir-frying is more about tossing and flipping than it is about stirring, so you want a sturdy tool to get the job done.

When using a wok, I recommend using a Chinese steel spatula, a wooden spatula or a heavy-duty plastic spatula.

If you're using a nonstick skillet, make sure to use a wooden or nonstick-safe plastic spatula, or else you'll scratch the skillet. If you're making multiple stir-fry dishes, plan ahead so you have a spatula at the ready for each dish.

Food Processor

I get by with a little help from my friends... but lately, my food processor has become my BFF and my cleaver is getting jealous! Because I'm always trying to squeeze as much

as possible into the day, I look for things to make life easier. Food processors can blend salad dressings, mince ginger, finely chop and grate vegetables, blend dumpling filling, and on and on. Go for a standard model and get the attachment blades so you can grate, shred and do other nifty stuff. Here's a fantastic time-saving tip my mom gave me for using a food processor for minced ginger: Peel about 1 lb (500 g) of fresh ginger and cut into medium pieces, then finely mince it in a food processor. Put the minced ginger in a resealable plastic storage bag and flatten it, then place it in the freezer. Once frozen, just break off what you need for your recipe!

Sauces

Imagine a world without a sweet-and-sour sauce to dip your crunchy egg roll into, or without a soy dipping sauce spiked with sesame oil and green onions to drizzle over your favorite dumplings at dim sum. Yes, I know, I'm painting a bleak and sad picture here, and I apologize. Chinese food just wouldn't be the same without its sauces.

This is a collection of some basic sauces and condiments, like Hoisin Sauce, which can be used to enhance flavors while cooking or to complement cooked food. I'm excited to share recipes for some of my mother's legendary sauces, like her earthy and spicy Chili Paste, bursting with umami goodness, and her Sweet Chili Soy Sauce, which delivers salty sweet heat in every bite. I also encourage you to try the Hot Chili Oil made with Sichuan peppercorns, which create an indescribable tingling sensation in your mouth and add an exotic note to this versatile condiment. It gives a sultry kick to anything you put it in.

This is just a sampling of some of my favorite sauces, but I hope you can gain the confidence to create your own sauces from scratch and make your world a better (and more delicious) place.

Sweet-and-Sour Sauce

My mother used to make this by the gallon for her catering business in our tiny basement in Minneapolis. On Saturday mornings, we would wake up not to the whiff of pancakes, but to the aroma of dark soy sauce, crushed pineapple and vinegar melding together to make this perfectly balanced dipping sauce that's just the right amount of sweet and just the right amount of sour. I always say life wouldn't be as sweet without the sour! This versatile sauce, also known as duck sauce or plum sauce, is great for everything from Chicken Egg Rolls (page 34) to Crab Wontons (page 44). For a quick and easy cocktail appetizer, cut some wonton wrappers into quarters, fry them up and serve them with this sauce.

Makes 5⅔ cups (1.25 liters)
Preparation time: 10 minutes
Cooking time: 8 minutes

One 20-oz (600-ml) can crushed pineapple
    in heavy syrup
1 cup (200 g) sugar
1 cup (250 ml) water
1 cup (250 ml) vinegar
1 tablespoon dark soy sauce
2 tablespoons all-purpose cornstarch
2 tablespoons cold water
1 cup (250 ml) plum sauce

1 Heat the pineapple (with syrup), sugar, 1 cup (250 ml) water, vinegar and soy sauce to boiling. Mix together the cornstarch and the 2 tablespoons cold water, then stir into the pineapple mixture. Heat to boiling, stirring constantly.

2 Remove from heat and cool to room temperature. Stir in the plum sauce. Cover and store in the refrigerator for up to two weeks.

COOK'S NOTE
Orange marmalade or plum jam can be substituted for plum sauce.

Sweet Chili Soy Sauce

My husband says this sauce is just like me: sweet, spicy, exotic and sometimes salty. Ha! I just love the sweet heat in this sauce, which is filled with piquant flavor and finishes with a fennel-like note from the star anise. Drizzle it over your favorite dumplings or steamed fish.

Makes 1 cup (250 ml)
Preparation time: 5 minutes
Cooking time: 30 minutes

¾ cup (185 ml) soy sauce
4 tablespoons water
½ cup (100 g) plus 1 tablespoon sugar
1 star anise pod
¼ teaspoon crushed red pepper

1 Combine the soy sauce, water, sugar, star anise and crushed red pepper in a small pan or skillet and mix with a fork or spoon.

2 Cook over low heat for 30 minutes, stirring occasionally. Remove from heat and discard the star anise.

3 Allow the sauce to cool for about an hour. Pour the cooled sauce into a jar with a tight-fitting lid. Use immediately or store in the refrigerator for up to 30 days.

Hoisin Sauce

My mother always taught me that of all the Chinese sauces, hoisin sauce is the boss. Why? Because of its versatility—it's used as a barbecue glaze, added to stir-fries, served as a dipping sauce and used in marinades. You can easily buy hoisin sauce at grocery stores, but I like to make it from scratch on Sunday afternoons when my kids are at soccer practice. Hoisin sauce is typically made with soybean paste, but I use peanut butter in this recipe for the sake of convenience.

Makes ¼ cup (65 ml)
Preparation time: 10 minutes

4 tablespoons soy sauce
2 tablespoons smooth peanut butter
1 tablespoon honey
2 teaspoons unseasoned rice vinegar
1 clove garlic, finely minced
2 teaspoons dark sesame oil
1 teaspoon Asian hot sauce, like Sriracha chili sauce
⅛ teaspoon white pepper

1 Combine all ingredients in a medium mixing bowl. Whisk until blended.

2 Transfer the sauce to a jar with a tight-fitting lid. Use immediately or store in the refrigerator for up to two weeks.

Hot Chili Oil

When my father used to bring us to visit Uncle Jack Yee at his eponymous Chinese restaurant in Hopkins, Minnesota, they'd sit in a corner reminiscing about China and playing cards. I remember the glistening jars of hot chili oil on the tables; their shimmering golden-red hue always looked like sunset in a jar to me. This seasoning oil is rich, layered, hot and complex. If you like things spicy, then this Sichuan classic will be your new go-to condiment. Have it by your stove to add a little kick to any stir-fry you're making, or drizzle it over roast chicken. It's even great on scrambled eggs. Hot chili oil should be used sparingly, as a little goes a long way.

Makes ¼ cup (65 ml)
Preparation time: 10 minutes + 8 to 10 hours resting time

6 tablespoons Sichuan peppercorns
One 1-in (2.5-cm) thick slice fresh ginger
2 star anise pods
½ cup (50 g) crushed red pepper
1 teaspoon salt
1 tablespoon dark sesame oil
4 tablespoons vegetable or canola oil

1 Place all of the ingredients, except the oils, in a medium glass bowl.

2 In a small saucepan, heat the oils to 375°F (190°C), then pour over the ingredients in the bowl. Let sit for 8 to 10 hours.

3 Strain the oil if you wish. Transfer to a glass jar with a tight-fitting lid and store in the refrigerator for up to two weeks.

Chili Paste

This is an earthy, rich paste that adds a spicy aromatic depth to any dish. It's more concentrated and hotter than chili garlic sauce. Whenever chili paste hit my mom's wok when we were growing up, its distinct aroma would wend its way up to my bedroom, and I knew we'd be gobbling up one of her amazing spicy dishes before long (she sure knew how to get me to finish my algebra!). You can buy chili paste at Asian markets, but it's easy-peasy to make, so I encourage you to try this at home.

Makes ½ cup (125 ml)
Preparation time: 10 minutes
Cooking time: 10 minutes

1 tablespoon oil
1 clove garlic, minced
1 teaspoon peeled and minced fresh ginger
½ cup (125 ml) brown bean paste
1 teaspoon ground red pepper (cayenne)
1 tablespoon sugar

1 Heat a wok or skillet on medium-low heat. Add all of the ingredients and cook for 10 minutes.

2 Allow the sauce to cool for about an hour. Pour the cooled sauce into a jar with a tight-fitting lid. Use immediately or store in the refrigerator for up to two weeks.

COOK'S NOTE
You may substitute hoisin sauce for the brown bean sauce, but if you do so, reduce the sugar to 1 teaspoon.

Starters and Dim Sum

D im sum, literally translated, means "to touch the heart," and it really does touch my heart to share some of my mother's recipes with you. I always smile when I think about dim sum because, other than its supreme deliciousness, it brings back memories of the time my mother and I went on *The Today Show* to make dim sum in celebration of Mother's Day and a Chinese steamed bun got stuck to Al Roker's face.

In this chapter, I share some of the dim sum we made during that appearance, as well as other classic gems such as Potstickers (page 28) and Crystal Shrimp Dumplings (page 30). I also share some of the yummy appetizers that we served in our catering business, like Firecracker Shrimp (page 43), which my clients called "Crack Shrimp" because they're so addicting. (My mother would say, "Why do they call it that? The shrimp isn't cracked.") Another popular appetizer on our menu was Edamame Hummus (page 49). It's fresh, light and gluten-free.

Of course, I couldn't leave out other classics, like crunchy Chicken Egg Rolls (page 34) and Crab Wontons (page 44), which my friend Mark describes as "soft pillows of heaven."

Make a selection of these recipes for your next get-together and I guarantee you'll "touch the heart" of all of your guests.

Potstickers

Also known as pan-fried dumplings and Peking ravioli, potstickers get their name from their crispy browned bottoms, which are achieved by the two-step cooking process of steaming followed by pan-frying. My mother and I used to teach people how to make this classic and beloved dumpling. Everyone would always "Ooh" and "Ahh" when they saw this cooking magic unfold before their very eyes. One of my favorite memories is of my mom teaching my twins how to make potstickers for Chinese New Year (their shape is similar to that of a gold ingot, so they symbolize prosperity). I couldn't believe how much fun they were having—plus, she got them to gobble up something that was stuffed with cabbage. Try adding spinach as another sneaky mom trick!

Serves 6 to 8 as an appetizer
or snack
Preparation time: 20 minutes
Cooking time: 10 minutes

4 oz (100 g) napa cabbage, cut
    into thin strips
1½ teaspoons salt, divided
8 oz (250 g) ground pork or
    chicken
2 tablespoons finely chopped
    green onion (scallion), white
    and green parts
2 teaspoons dry white wine
½ teaspoon all-purpose
    cornstarch
½ teaspoon dark sesame oil
Dash of white pepper
20 to 30 potsticker wrappers
2 to 4 tablespoons oil for frying

DIPPING SAUCE

4 tablespoons soy sauce
1 teaspoon dark sesame oil
½ teaspoon sugar

1 Toss the cabbage with 1 teaspoon of the salt and set aside for 5 minutes, then roll the cabbage up in a clean dry dish towel. Twist the dish towel to squeeze out the excess moisture.

2 In a large bowl, mix the cabbage, pork or chicken, green onion, wine, cornstarch, sesame oil, the remaining ½ teaspoon salt and the pepper.

3 Lay a potsticker wrapper on a clean work surface. Place 1 tablespoon of the meat mixture in the center. Lift up the edges of the circle and pinch several pleats up to create a pouch encasing the mixture. Pinch the top together. Repeat with the remaining wrappers and filling.

4 Heat 1 tablespoon of the oil for frying in a wok or skillet over moderately high heat. Place 12 dumplings in a single layer in the wok or skillet and fry 2 minutes, or until the bottoms are golden brown. Add ½ cup (125 ml) water.

5 Cover and cook for 6 to 7 minutes, or until the water is absorbed. Repeat with the remaining dumplings.

6 Make the dipping sauce: Combine the soy sauce, sesame oil and sugar. Serve alongside the dumplings.

COOK'S NOTE
If you can't find round dumpling wrappers,
you can substitute square wonton wrappers.
Just use a cookie cutter to cut them into
rounds.

Toss the cabbage with 1 teaspoon of salt and set aside for 5 minutes.

Roll the cabbage up in a clean dry dish towel. Twist the towel to squeeze out the excess moisture.

Mix the dumpling ingredients together in a bowl.

Place 1 tablespoon of the meat mixture in the center of a dumpling wrapper.

Lift the edges and pinch several pleats to create a pouch for the mixture. Pinch the top together.

Repeat with the remaining wrappers and filling.

Heat oil in a wok or skillet. Place 12 dumplings in a single layer and fry for 2 minutes, or until the bottoms are golden brown.

Add ½ cup (125 ml) of water. Cover and cook 6 to 7 minutes or until the water is absorbed. Repeat with the remaining dumplings.

Crystal Shrimp Dumplings

My mother and I were asked to teach a dim sum class where we demonstrated these light and flavorful dumplings. Our students couldn't believe how easy they are to make using such simple ingredients. In fact, this is the type of recipe you can whip up for unexpected guests within minutes if you have frozen shrimp and dumpling wrappers in your freezer (always a good idea). When cooking for guests, I'd double or triple the batch, as these dumplings tend to fly right off the plate. Not only will your guests be impressed, you'll get down with your bad self.

Serves 6 to 8 as an appetizer or snack
Preparation time: 20 minutes
Cooking time: 3 to 4 minutes

COOK'S NOTE
If you only can find square dumpling wrappers, use a cookie cutter to cut them into rounds.

8 oz (250 g) shelled and deveined medium-sized raw shrimp
¼ teaspoon salt
½ teaspoon sugar
Dash of white pepper
½ teaspoon dark sesame oil
1 teaspoon all-purpose cornstarch
1 egg white, divided in two portions
4 tablespoons finely chopped fresh coriander leaves (cilantro)
20 store-bought round dumpling wrappers
1 tablespoon oil
½ cup (125 ml) water

DIPPING SAUCE

2 tablespoons soy sauce
2 tablespoons balsamic vinegar
1 tablespoon chopped green onion (scallion), white and green parts

1 Follow the directions for "Eliminating Shrimp's 'Fishy' Taste" on page 20. (This step is optional.)

2 To make the filling, first chop the shrimp into a paste with a knife or a food processor.

3 In a medium bowl, combine the shrimp, salt, sugar, pepper, sesame oil, cornstarch, ½ egg white and cilantro.

4 In a separate small bowl, beat the remaining ½ egg white with 1 tablespoon water for sealing the dumplings.

5 Make the dipping sauce: Mix the soy sauce, balsamic vinegar and green onion. Set aside.

6 Place 2 teaspoons of the filling in the center of each dumpling wrapper. Brush with the egg mixture along the edge. Fold over to form a half-circle.

7 Heat the oil in a wok or skillet over medium-high heat. Add all of the dumplings and pan-fry for 1 minute.

8 Add the water. Cover and cook for 1 minute, then remove the cover and continue to cook until the water is completely gone, about 2 minutes. Serve immediately with the dipping sauce.

Veggie Tofu Lettuce Cups

When my friend Stacy tried this recipe, she couldn't believe her teenage daughters, Brianna and McKenna, were devouring tofu and liking it. It takes a little extra time to prepare and bake the tofu, but it's totally worth it. I love the combination of textures that the water chestnuts and shiitake mushrooms contribute, but the sauce, which is rich and layered from the dark soy sauce, hoisin sauce and rice wine, is the best part. This is a great appetizer for "Meatless Mondays"—it's even hearty enough for dinner with a side of Egg Drop Soup (page 64).

Serves 6 to 8 as an appetizer or snack
Preparation time: 20 minutes + draining and marinating time
Cooking time: 45 minutes

One 16-oz (500 g) block firm tofu, drained

MARINADE

⅓ cup (80 ml) soy sauce
¾ cup (185 ml) water
1 tablespoon peeled and minced fresh ginger
3 cloves garlic, minced
1½ tablespoons dark sesame oil

2 tablespoons oil
1 tablespoon finely chopped shallot
1 tablespoon peeled and minced fresh ginger
1 fresh hot red chili (deseeded if you prefer less heat)
4 tablespoons water chestnuts, finely chopped
2½ cups (250 g) fresh shiitake mushrooms, chopped
4 tablespoons green onion (scallion), finely chopped (green and white parts)
4 tablespoons Chinese rice wine or sherry
1 tablespoon dark soy sauce
1 tablespoon hoisin sauce, homemade (page 25) or store-bought
Leaves of 1 head butter lettuce, washed and dried

1 Preheat oven to 400°F (200°C).

2 Wrap tofu block snugly in 4 or 5 layers of paper towels and place on a plate. Cover with a second plate and balance a heavy can or two on top to weigh down the plate and press down on the tofu. Set aside to let drain for 30 minutes. Remove and discard paper towels, then replace with dry paper towels and repeat the process a second time. Cut the pressed tofu into 1-inch (2.5 cm) cubes.

3 Whisk marinade ingredients together in a medium bowl. Add the tofu cubes and gently toss to coat. Cover and place in refrigerator for 30 minutes.

4 Arrange tofu cubes in a single layer on a large sheet pan lined with parchment paper. Lightly spray tofu all over with cooking spray and bake, flipping halfway through, until golden brown and just crisp, about 40 minutes total.

5 Heat the oil in a wok or skillet over medium-high heat. Add the shallot, ginger and chili and stir-fry until fragrant. Add the water chestnuts, shiitake mushrooms and green onions and stir-fry for 2 minutes. Add the tofu and stir-fry for 1 minute, then pour in the soy sauce, rice wine or sherry and hoisin sauce and stir-fry for another minute.

6 Transfer to a serving bowl. Place the lettuce leaves on a plate or platter alongside the tofu filling so guests can make their own wraps.

Shiitake Mushroom and Spinach Dumplings

When I brought my vegetarian friend Dave to dim sum for the first time, he was pleasantly surprised to see the array of meatless dumpling options going around in the carts. All of my non-Chinese friends make me do the ordering at dim sum (even though I can't even speak Chinese!), and I load up on as many veggie dumplings as I do the meat or seafood kind, because they're so healthy, fresh and flavorful. This recipe, loaded with umami flavor from the shiitakes, is inspired by one of my favorite veggie dumplings at my go-to dim sum restaurant, Ocean Seafood, in Los Angeles' Chinatown.

Serves 8 as an appetizer or snack
Preparation time: 25 minutes
Cooking time: 4 minutes

8 oz (250 g) firm tofu
2 egg whites, divided
2 teaspoons peeled and minced fresh ginger
1 clove garlic, minced
2 tablespoons finely chopped green onion (scallion),
  white and green parts
1 tablespoon soy sauce
½ teaspoon dark sesame oil
1 teaspoon all-purpose cornstarch
2 tablespoons finely chopped fresh coriander leaves
  (cilantro)
½ cup (50 g) stemmed and finely chopped fresh
  shiitake mushrooms
4 tablespoons thawed frozen spinach, squeezed dry
  and finely chopped
30 store-bought round potsticker wrappers
3 tablespoons oil, divided, for frying
Water, for cooking

DIPPING SAUCE

2 tablespoons soy sauce
2 tablespoons balsamic vinegar
1 teaspoon green onion (scallion), finely chopped
  (green and white parts)

1 Drain the tofu and pat dry, then dice finely.

2 In a large bowl, combine one of the egg whites, the ginger, garlic, green onion, soy sauce, sesame oil, cornstarch, coriander leaves, mushrooms and spinach until blended. Add the tofu and toss gently into mixture.

3 Make the dipping sauce: Combine the soy sauce and balsamic vinegar in a small bowl. Sprinkle green onion on top and set aside.

4 Beat the remaining egg white with 2 teaspoons water. Lay one potsticker wrapper on a clean work surface, and place 2 teaspoons of the filling in the center of the circle. Brush egg white mixture along the edge of the wrapper, then fold over to form a half-circle and seal the dumpling shut. Repeat with remaining ingredients.

5 Heat a large skillet over high heat. Add 1 tablespoon of the oil and reduce the heat to medium. Add 10 dumplings and pan-fry for 1 minute. Add 4 tablespoons water, then cover and cook for 1 minute more.

6 Remove the cover and continue to cook until the water is gone, about 2 minutes. Repeat the process until all the dumplings are cooked. Serve immediately with the dipping sauce alongside.

COOK'S NOTE
*If you only can find square dumpling wrappers,
use a cookie cutter to cut them into rounds.*

Chicken Egg Rolls

A lot of my friends outside of New York complain that they can't find their beloved New York–style egg rolls anywhere else. These egg rolls, made with the thicker, egg-based wrappers which bubble on the outside when you cook them, are filled with succulent chicken and bean sprouts seasoned with a bit of five-spice powder. I remember when my parents drove us to Manhattan in their Chevy station wagon in the 1970s to visit my oldest sister, Linda. Once we arrived in the city, we headed straight to New York's Chinatown for dinner. Being from Minnesota, I had never seen so many Chinese people in one place at once! My mom's delicious egg roll recipe reminds me of that trip, and of all the times she made these for us.

Serves 6 to 8 as an appetizer or snack
Preparation time: 15 minutes + soaking time
Cooking time: 4 to 6 minutes

2 or 3 dried black mushrooms
1 lb (500 g) boneless, skinless chicken breast,
  cut into thin strips
1½ teaspoons salt, divided
½ teaspoon all-purpose cornstarch
4 tablespoons oil, divided
1 lb (500 g) bean sprouts, ends trimmed
1 teaspoon five-spice powder
4 tablespoons canned bamboo shoots, shredded
4 tablespoons chopped green onion (scallion),
  green and white parts
Store-bought egg roll wrappers
1 egg, beaten
Oil for deep-frying
Sweet-and-Sour Sauce (page 24)

COOK'S NOTE
You can freeze cooked egg rolls once they've cooled. To use, simply heat oven to 425°F (220°C) and bake the frozen egg rolls on a cookie sheet for 25 to 30 minutes, until hot and crispy.

1 Soak the mushrooms in warm water until soft, about 30 minutes. Rinse in warm water and drain. Remove and discard the stems and shred the caps.

2 Mix the chicken, ½ teaspoon of the salt and the cornstarch. Set aside.

3 Heat 2 tablespoons of the oil in a wok or skillet over medium-high heat. Add the bean sprouts and stir-fry for 2 minutes. Combine the remaining teaspoon of salt and the five-spice powder in a small bowl. Stir half of the mixture into the bean sprouts, then remove the bean sprouts from the pan.

4 Add the remaining 2 tablespoons oil to the wok or skillet. Add the chicken and stir-fry until chicken turns white. Add the mushrooms and bamboo shoots and stir-fry for 2 minutes. Stir in the bean sprouts, the remaining five-spice mixture and the green onion. Transfer to a strainer and drain thoroughly. Let cool.

5 To prepare the egg rolls, lay one egg roll wrapper onto a clean work surface (cover the remaining wrappers with a dampened towel to keep them pliable). Place ½ cup (50 g) of the egg roll filling slightly below the center of the wrapper. Fold the bottom corner of the egg roll wrapper over the filling, tucking the point under. Fold in and overlap the two opposite corners. Brush the fourth corner with egg and roll up the enclosed filling to seal. Repeat with remaining egg roll wrappers.

6 In a large wok or deep skillet, heat 2 to 3 inches (5 to 7.5 cm) of the oil to 350°F (175°C). Fry 4 or 5 egg rolls at a time until golden brown, about 2 or 3 minutes per side, turning twice or three times. Drain on a sheet pan lined with paper towels. Serve immediately with Sweet-and-Sour Sauce.

Shu Mai

Oh my, Shu Mai! This is my favorite dim sum dumpling because it's so yummy, healthy (it's steamed) and cute. My mother was an incredible seamstress, on top of being a master chef, so she made the pleating on her shu mai look effortless. It has taken me, however, several years to perfect my *shu mai* pleating. In fact, my mother once asked me, "Why are you so slow?" on camera while I was making *shu mai* for a Food Network special in China. She was hard on me, but it was always out of love. Anyway, practice makes perfect—and the great thing about Chinese dumplings is that no matter how they look, they always taste delicious! Filled with tender chicken and shrimp, with little bursts of ginger and onion, this open-faced steamed dumpling is a family favorite.

Serves 6 to 8 as an appetizer or snack
Preparation time: 15 minutes + mushroom soaking time
Cooking time: 12 minutes

4 medium dried black mushrooms
8 oz (250 g) shelled and deveined medium-sized raw shrimp
⅛ teaspoon white pepper
½ teaspoon dark sesame oil
½ egg white
1 tablespoon all-purpose cornstarch
2 teaspoons oil
½ teaspoon salt
1 teaspoon peeled and minced fresh ginger
2 tablespoons finely chopped carrot
4 tablespoons finely chopped onion
10 oz (330 g) ground chicken breast
18 round dumpling wrappers

DIPPING SAUCE

3 tablespoons soy sauce
½ teaspoon sugar
1 tablespoon water
1 tablespoon chopped green onion (scallion), white and
  green parts

1 Soak the mushrooms in hot water for 15 to 20 minutes, or until soft. Rinse them in cold water and drain. Squeeze out any excess water. Remove and discard the stems and cut the mushrooms into ¼ inch (6 mm) pieces.

2 Follow the directions for "Eliminating Shrimp's 'Fishy' Taste" on page 20. (This step is optional.) Chop the shrimp finely.

3 In a medium bowl, combine the pepper, sesame oil, egg white, cornstarch, oil, salt, ginger, carrot and onion. Add the chicken, shrimp and mushrooms; mix very well and set aside.

4 Make the dipping sauce: In a small bowl, whisk together the soy sauce, sugar, water and chopped green onion. Set aside.

5 Lay a dumpling wrapper on a clean work surface. Place 1 tablespoon of the chicken and shrimp mixture in the center of a wrapper. Bring the edges up around the filling, pinching and pleating as you go, leaving the top open. Repeat with the remaining wrappers.

6 Place the dumplings in a single layer on a rack in a steamer. Cover and steam over boiling water for 12 minutes. (Add additional boiling water during steaming if necessary.)

COOK'S NOTE
To freeze Shu Mai, steam them and let them cool completely. Place the dumplings in a large resealable food storage bag for freezing. To use, let them thaw and then steam them for 6 minutes, or pop them in the microwave for 4 to 5 minutes.

Whisk together the dipping sauce ingredients in a small bowl.

Combine the shu mai filling ingredients in a medium bowl.

Place 1 tablespoon of the chicken and shrimp mixture in the center of a wrapper.

Bring the edges up around the filling, pinching and pleating as you go, leaving the top open.

Peking Duck Summer Rolls

If you know anything about making Peking duck, you know it takes a commitment of time and energy: you need to blow up the duck with a bicycle pump and then let it air-dry overnight. (When we were growing up in Minnesota, my mother would hang ducks up to dry in our kitchen window, overlooking our driveway. Neighborhood kids bicycling up and down our driveway would see the ducks and scream, and then pedal away as fast as they could!) I wanted to recreate the flavor and texture of this famous dish without requiring all the effort and time. In this recipe I use duck breast which is marinated, roasted and then flash-fried to achieve a crispy skin; it's then wrapped in rice-paper wrappers. I was inspired to try this modern take on Peking duck during a trip to Hong Kong my mother and I took one year to judge a cooking competition. It's tender, juicy and oh, so delicious topped with hoisin sauce and green onions.

Serves 6 to 8 as an appetizer or snack
Preparation time: 20 minutes + marinating time
Cooking time: 30 minutes

MARINADE
4 tablespoons hoisin sauce, homemade (page 25) or store-bought
3 cloves garlic, minced
1 teaspoon five-spice powder
2 tablespoons soy sauce
2 tablespoons sugar
2 teaspoons rice vinegar or white vinegar
2 tablespoons Chinese rice wine or sherry

1 lb (500 g) boneless duck breast, skin intact
2 tablespoons oil
1 package 12-in (30-cm) round rice paper wrappers
⅓ cup (80 ml) hoisin sauce, homemade (page 25) or store-bought
2 green onions (scallions), cut into shreds (green and white parts)
1 cucumber, peeled and deseeded, cut into 3-in (7.5-cm) thin strips

1 In a small bowl, whisk together the marinade ingredients, then pour into a resealable plastic food-storage bag. Add the duck breast to the bag and place in the refrigerator for at least 30 minutes and up to 2 hours.

2 Preheat oven to 400°F (200°C).

3 Remove the duck breast from the marinade and transfer to a sheet pan. Roast for 25 to 30 minutes. Remove from oven and allow to rest for 10 minutes.

4 Heat the oil in a skillet over medium-high heat. Add the duck breast, skin-side down, and cook for 3 to 5 minutes, or until the skin is crisp. Drain on a sheet pan lined with paper towels. Allow to rest for 3 to 5 minutes, then slice thinly and place on a serving platter.

5 Fill a shallow bowl with warm water, making sure it is large enough to fit the rice paper wrappers. Lay a clean towel on your work surface. Carefully dip a rice paper wrapper into the water, just to get it wet all over. Try not to crack it, as it will still be slightly hard. Remove it from the water and lay it on the clean towel, where it will continue to soften.

6 To roll, spread 1 teaspoon of the hoisin sauce on the bottom third of the rice paper wrapper. Place about 3 slices of duck on top of the sauce. Add some cucumber strips and green onion shreds. Roll the wrapper all the way up. Repeat the procedure with remaining ingredients. Serve immediately.

Pour the marinade into a food-storage bag. Add the duck to the bag. Refrigerate for 30 minutes.

Allow the duck breasts to rest for 10 minutes after roasting.

Carefully dip a rice paper wrapper into warm water, then lay it onto a clean towel.

Add the contents of the roll to the rice paper wrapper, then begin to roll it up.

Continue rolling all the way up.

Spicy Beef Skewers

When I first moved to Los Angeles eons ago, I brought my mom to Koreatown. She tried Korean barbecue for the first time and fell in love! In our catering business, we wanted to add some Korean flavors to this classic Chinese beef preparation, so we threw in some sugar and ground red pepper. This gives these incredibly flavorful and tender skewers a sweet and spicy finish. They're also great for a cocktail party, because you can marinate them the night before and just throw them on the grill a few minutes before your guests arrive. Soaking the beef in baking soda and water tenderizes the beef, making for melt-in-your-mouth results.

Serves 3 to 5 as an appetizer or snack
Preparation time: 20 minutes + soaking and marinating time
Cooking time: 4 to 5 minutes

1 tablespoon baking soda
2 cups (500 ml) water
1½ lbs (750 g) beef flank steak
20 wooden skewers, soaked in water for 30 minutes

MARINADE

2 tablespoons oil
1 teaspoon soy sauce
1 teaspoon salt
1 tablespoon (about 3 cloves) minced garlic
1 tablespoon peeled and minced fresh ginger
1 teaspoon sugar
1 teaspoon ground red pepper (cayenne)
2 tablespoons all-purpose cornstarch
4 tablespoons hoisin sauce, homemade (page 25) or store-bought

1 In a large flat pan, dissolve the baking soda in the water. Add the beef and soak for 10 minutes. Remove the beef from the water and pat dry with paper towels. Cut the beef into thin strips across the grain.

2 Whisk together all marinade ingredients in a large mixing bowl. Place beef strips in a large resealable food storage bag and pour the marinade over. Refrigerate for at least 30 minutes, or as long as overnight.

3 Thread the beef strips onto the soaked skewers.

4 Preheat broiler. Broil the meat about 4 inches (10 cm) from the heat for about 2 minutes. Turn the skewers over and broil for another 2 minutes.

COOK'S NOTE
You can use the baking soda and water tenderizing technique for any beef dish. Use approximately 1 teaspoon baking soda and 2 cups (500 ml) water per 8 oz (250 g) of beef, and soak for 10 minutes.

Honey Barbecued Pork

Honey, have I got a surprise for you! The honey in this Honey Barbecued Pork recipe creates an amazing sweet glaze. The five-spice powder adds sweetness and complexity, and a bit of brandy gives this Chinese classic depth and an edge. Slice this up for sandwiches (I love using store-bought Peking duck buns) or throw a few slices into some wonton soup. While the other kids had hot dogs, my mom used to bring slices of Honey Barbecued Pork for our picnics at Lake Harriet in Minneapolis.

Serves 4 to 6 as an appetizer or snack
Preparation time: 15 minutes + marinating time
Cooking time: 40 minutes

1½ lbs (750 g) boneless pork butt or shoulder, trimmed of fat

MARINADE
2 tablespoons ketchup
1 teaspoon salt
2 teaspoons sugar
1 clove garlic, minced
1 teaspoon brandy
½ teaspoon five-spice powder
4 tablespoons honey

1 In a small bowl, combine the ketchup, salt, sugar, garlic, brandy, five-spice powder and honey. Rub this mixture on the pork, covering all sides. Reserve any leftover sauce for serving. Marinate the pork in the refrigerator, covered, for at least 2 hours.

2 Preheat oven to 425°F (220°C).

3 Place the pork on a rack in a roasting pan and roast for 20 minutes. Turn over and return to oven for an additional 20 minutes. Reduce heat to 350°F (175°C) and cook for an additional 20 minutes, until the pork reaches an internal temperature of 170°F (80°C).

4 Remove from the oven. When the pork is cool enough to handle, cut across the grain into pieces ¼ inch (6 mm) thick. Serve at room temperature or cold. Brush any leftover marinade sauce over the sliced pork before serving.

Tofu Bites with Three Sauces

Three is a luckier number in Chinese than four. Four is unlucky, which is why you typically never see four items in a steamer basket at a dim sum restaurant (check this out the next time you go for dim sum). When I was developing this recipe a few months ago, I started with four sauces, but then I heard my mother's voice in my head about the number four: "Don't rent that #4 apartment!" I hope these crispy tofu nuggets—crunchy on the outside, but soft and creamy on the inside—bring you luck with their three delicious dipping sauces. The Sriracha Mayo delivers a creamy heat, while the Soy Balsamic is sweet-tart and salty, and the Hoisin Peanut is rich and nutty. This appetizer is also a vegetarian delight!

Serves 6 to 8 as an appetizer or snack
Preparation time: 45 minutes
Cooking time: 10 minutes

SRIRACHA-MAYO SAUCE

½ cup (120 g) mayonnaise
1 tablespoon Sriracha chili sauce
½ teaspoon freshly squeezed lime juice

SOY-BALSAMIC SAUCE

2 tablespoons soy sauce
2 tablespoons balsamic vinegar
1 teaspoon green onion (scallion),
   finely chopped

HOISIN-PEANUT SAUCE

½ cup (125 ml) hoisin sauce, homemade
   (page 25) or store-bought
2 tablespoons smooth peanut butter
2 tablespoons water
1 tablespoon rice vinegar or white vinegar
Crushed roasted peanuts for garnish

2 tablespoons flour
2 tablespoons all-purpose cornstarch
1 teaspoon five-spice powder
½ teaspoon salt
8 oz (225 g) firm tofu, drained, patted dry
   and cut into cubes
Oil for deep-frying

1 Make the Sriracha-Mayo Sauce: Mix the mayonnaise, Sriracha and lime juice together in a small bowl until blended. Set aside.

2 Make the Soy-Balsamic Sauce: Mix the soy sauce and balsamic vinegar in a small bowl until blended and garnish with green onion. Set aside.

3 Make the Hoisin-Peanut Sauce: Bring the hoisin sauce, peanut butter, water and vinegar to a boil in a saucepan over moderately high heat. Immediately remove from the heat and transfer to a small serving bowl. Garnish with crushed peanuts. Set aside.

4 Combine the flour, cornstarch, five-spice powder and salt in a bowl. Toss the tofu pieces in the flour mixture.

5 In a large wok or deep skillet, heat 2 to 3 inches (5 to 7.5 cm) of the oil to 350°F (175°C). Fry the tofu for 3 to 4 minutes. Turn and fry for another 3 to 4 minutes, until golden brown all over. Drain on a sheet pan lined with paper towels. Transfer to a platter and serve immediately with dipping sauces.

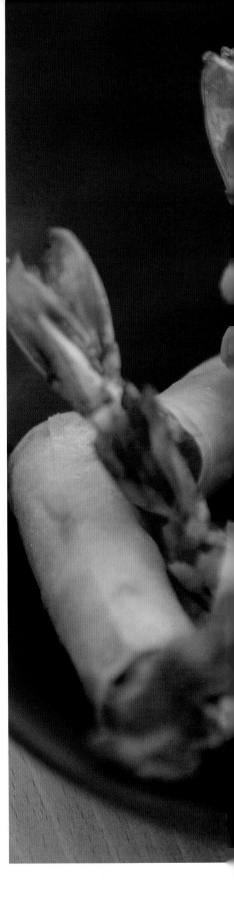

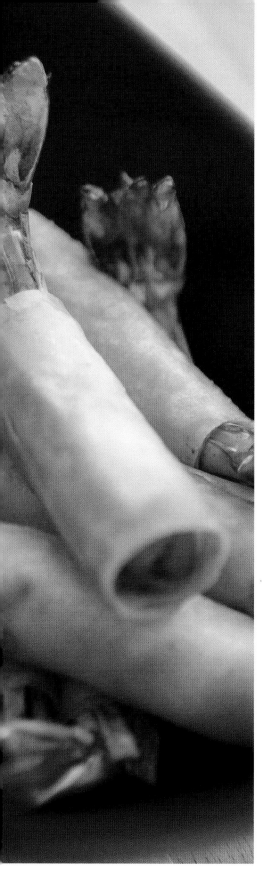

Firecracker Shrimp

Growing up, Chinese New Year was my favorite time of year. My mother and father would lay out brand new outfits and shoes for us to wear so we could start the New Year off fresh, and we couldn't wash our hair on Chinese New Year's day or else we'd wash out all of our good luck. My mother explained all of the symbolism of the foods we ate on this day to bring fortune, honor, health and good luck into our homes. She told us about the firecrackers on New Year's Day in China when she was a little girl, and how they lit up the sky to ward off evil spirits. Together, my mom and I came up with this fun and festive recipe that's great for Chinese New Year, or any time of the year when you want a little good luck. The carrot resembles the fuse of a firecracker!

Serves 6 as an appetizer or snack
Preparation time: 10 minutes
Cooking time: 2 minutes

12 shelled (tail left intact) and deveined large raw shrimp
½ teaspoon garlic salt, divided
4 spring roll wrappers
1 large carrot, cut into 3 x ¼-in (7.5 x 6-mm) matchsticks
1 egg, beaten
Oil for deep-frying

DIPPING SAUCE

4 tablespoons mayonnaise
2 tablespoons Sriracha chili sauce

1 Follow the directions for "Eliminating Shrimp's 'Fishy' Taste" on page 20. (This step is optional.)

2 Cut each spring roll wrapper into thirds to make 12 long narrow strips.

3 Place the carrot slices in a small bowl. Sprinkle with ¼ teaspoon of the garlic salt and set aside. Sprinkle the shrimp with the remaining garlic salt.

4 Brush the top third of each spring roll strip with egg. Place a piece of shrimp at the bottom of the strip. Place a carrot slice on top of the shrimp. Roll each shrimp and carrot up tightly in the spring roll strip, with the egg holding it together. The tail of the shrimp and the carrot should be protruding from one end to resemble a firecracker. Repeat the process until all the wrappers are filled with the shrimp and carrots.

5 Make the dipping sauce: In a small bowl, mix the mayonnaise and Sriracha sauce together. Set aside.

6 In a large wok or deep skillet, heat 2 to 3 inches (5 to 7.5 cm) of the oil to 350°F (175°C). Fry the shrimp rolls until golden brown, about 2 minutes, turning 2 to 3 times. Drain on a sheet pan lined with paper towels. Serve with the dipping sauce.

Crispy Wontons

When my mother began making a name for herself as a caterer in the late 1970s, she met Sean Connery, who became an investor in her first restaurant. Sean brought Robert Redford to a party she was catering. I was a server at the party (my mother believed in Chinese child labor) and in all my preteen awkwardness and braces, I walked up to him with a platter of my mother's delicious wontons. Knees buckling, I said, "Would you like a Chinese wonton, Mr. Redford?" He couldn't have been kinder or handsomer. After biting into one of my mother's tender, juicy wontons filled with chicken and water chestnuts, he said, "Delish," and gave me wink.

Serves 6 to 8 as an appetizer or snack
Preparation time: 20 minutes
Cooking time: 3 to 4 minutes

8 oz (250 g) shelled and deveined medium-size shrimp, finely chopped
4 oz (100 g) ground chicken or pork
6 canned water chestnuts, finely chopped
4 tablespoons finely chopped green onion (scallion), white and green parts
1 teaspoon all-purpose cornstarch
1 teaspoon salt
⅛ teaspoon dark sesame oil
Dash of white pepper
20 Wonton wrappers
1 large egg, slightly beaten
Oil for frying
Sweet-and-Sour Sauce (page 24)

1 Follow the directions for "Eliminating Shrimp's 'Fishy' Taste" on page 20. (This step is optional).

2 In a medium bowl, combine the shrimp, chicken or pork, water chestnuts, green onion, cornstarch, salt, sesame oil and white pepper.

3 Lay a wonton wrapper on a clean work surface (cover remaining wrappers with plastic wrap to keep them pliable). Place ½ teaspoon of the shrimp mixture in the center. Fold the wonton wrapper over the filling to form a triangle, then turn the top of the triangle over to meet the folded edge. Turn over; moisten one corner with beaten egg. Overlap the two corners so that the moistened side is between them and press together firmly. Repeat with the remaining wrappers.

4 In a large wok or deep skillet, heat 2 to 3 inches (5 to 7.5 cm) of the oil to 350°F (175°C). Fry 8 to 10 wontons at a time, turning 2 or 3 times, until golden brown, about 3 minutes. Drain on a sheet pan lined with paper towels. Serve immediately, accompanied by Sweet-and-Sour Sauce.

COOK'S NOTE
You can find wonton wrappers at an Asian market, as well as in the produce or fresh pasta section of most large grocery stores.

Crab Wontons

No one knows the exact origin of these Crab Wontons, otherwise known as Crab Rangoon or Crab Puffs, but they were popularized by Polynesian restaurants. All I know is that when my mother introduced these pillows of creamy crabmeat heaven in her restaurants, people went wild—so wild, in fact, that she eventually took out the crab and just made them with cream cheese!

Serves 6 to 8 as an appetizer or snack
Preparation time: 15 minutes
Cooking time: 5 minutes

6 oz (175 g) crabmeat, picked through for shells
Two 8-oz (250-g) packages cream cheese,
   softened
½ teaspoon salt
¼ teaspoon garlic powder
20 wonton wrappers
1 egg, slightly beaten
Oil for frying
Sweet-and-Sour Sauce (page 24)

1 In a medium bowl, mix together the crabmeat, cream cheese, salt and garlic powder until well combined.

2 Lay one wonton wrapper on a clean work surface (cover remaining wrappers with plastic wrap to keep them pliable). Brush the edges of the wrappers with beaten egg, then place a heaping teaspoonful of crabmeat mixture in the center. Fold the bottom corner of the wonton wrapper over the filling to form a triangle and seal the edges. Pinch the two folded corners together. Repeat with the remaining wrappers.

3 In a large wok or deep skillet, heat 2 to 3 inches (5 to 7.5 cm) of the oil to 350°F (175°C). Fry 8 to 10 wontons at a time, turning 2 or 3 times, until golden brown, about 2 minutes. Drain on a sheet pan lined with paper towels. Serve immediately with Sweet-and-Sour Sauce.

COOK'S NOTE
Imitation crab sticks can be substituted for crabmeat if you prefer.

Paper-Wrapped Chicken

Who doesn't like receiving a package? I remember how excited my siblings and I were whenever our parents ordered this Chinese appetizer for us at restaurants. Not only did we each get our own individual packet to open up, but inside were juicy, tender pieces of chicken marinated in white wine, ginger, sesame oil and dark soy sauce. The flavorings are trapped in the packets along with the chicken while it's cooking, so the meat is incredibly succulent and flavorful. When we got older, we begged our mom to show us how to make it. This appetizer, a retro classic, doesn't appear on Chinese restaurant menus as often as it used to, so I wanted to bring it back as my special wrapped gift to you. You won't unwrap a more delicious present!

Serves 6 to 8 as an appetizer or snack
Preparation time: 15 minutes + marinating time
Cooking time: 15 minutes

3 lbs (1.5 kg) boneless, skinless chicken breast, cut into 1½ x ½-in (5 x 1.25-cm) strips
1 tablespoon oil
2 teaspoons dry white wine
1 teaspoon all-purpose cornstarch
1 teaspoon peeled and minced fresh ginger
1 teaspoon salt
1 teaspoon dark soy sauce
½ teaspoon sugar
¼ teaspoon white pepper
¼ teaspoon dark sesame oil
Thirty 6-in (15-cm) squares aluminum foil, parchment or waxed paper
Oil for pan-frying

1 Toss the chicken, oil, wine, cornstarch, ginger, salt, soy sauce, sugar, white pepper and sesame oil together in a glass or plastic bowl. Cover and refrigerate for 1 hour.

2 Lay one square of foil or paper on a clean work surface. Place 2 strips of chicken slightly below the center of the square. Fold the nearest corner over the chicken. Fold up again. Overlap the two opposing corners. Fold the fourth corner down and tuck it under overlapping corners, making sure the chicken is securely sealed in foil. Repeat with remaining wrapping squares.

3 In a large wok or deep skillet, heat 1½ inches (4 cm) of oil to 350°F (175°C). Fry 10 packets at a time, turning 3 or 4 times, for about 3 minutes. Drain on a sheet pan lined with a paper towel. Transfer to a platter and serve immediately.

COOK'S NOTE
If you prefer to bake the packets instead of deep-frying them, bake for 15 minutes in a 350°F (175°C) oven.

Toss chicken and the other ingredients into a bowl. Cover and refrigerate 1 hour.

Fold the corner of the square closest to the chicken over the chicken. Fold up again.

The corners are now folded in.

Fry 10 packets at a time.

Place two strips of chicken slightly below the center of a parchment paper square.

Overlap the two opposite corners until secure.

Fold the fourth corner down and tuck it under the overlapping corners.

Remove from oil immediately and drain on a sheet pan lined with paper towel.

Chicken Skewers

I always make Chicken Skewers when I'm entertaining, because I know my low carb/no carb friends (remember, I do live in LA) will love them as much as everyone else. If I'm cooking for gluten-free friends, I just swap out the soy sauce for tamari, which is gluten free. It's easy to overcook chicken, so keep your eye on the skewers. You can marinate the meat in the refrigerator all day until you're ready to cook that night. If you have leftovers, cut up the pieces of chicken and toss them with mixed greens for lunch the next day.

Serves 6 as an appetizer or snack
Preparation Time: 15 minutes + 30 minutes (or more) for marinating
Cooking time: 5 minutes

1 tablespoon oil
2 teaspoons dry white wine
1 teaspoon peeled and minced fresh ginger
1 teaspoon all-purpose cornstarch
1 teaspoon salt
1 teaspoon dark soy sauce
1 teaspoon sugar
¼ teaspoon white pepper
¼ teaspoon dark sesame oil
1 lb (500 g) skinless, boneless chicken
   breast or chicken thigh, cut into strips
14 wooden skewers, soaked in
   water for 30 minutes

DIPPING SAUCE
2 tablespoons hoisin sauce, homemade
   (page 25) or store-bought
1 tablespoon unseasoned rice vinegar
1 teaspoon dark sesame oil
1 tablespoon soy sauce
2 tablespoons water
1 tablespoon oil
2 tablespoons peeled and minced fresh
   ginger
2 cloves garlic, minced
2 tablespoons finely chopped fresh
   coriander leaves (cilantro)

1 In a small bowl, whisk together the oil, wine, ginger, cornstarch, salt, soy sauce, sugar, pepper and sesame oil. Add the chicken and stir until combined. Cover and refrigerate for at least 30 minutes, or as long as overnight.

2 Make the dipping sauce: Mix the hoisin sauce, rice vinegar, sesame oil, soy sauce, and water in a small bowl. Heat the oil in a small saucepan over medium-high heat. Add the ginger and garlic and stir-fry until fragrant, about 30 seconds. Stir in the hoisin mixture and cook for 2–3 minutes. Remove from heat and stir in the fresh coriander leaves.

3 Preheat broiler. Meanwhile, thread the chicken pieces onto the soaked skewers.

4 Broil the skewers about 4 inches (10 cm) from the heat, turning once, until done, about 5 minutes. Serve immediately with the dipping sauce.

Edamame Hummus

In the midst of running our catering business together, my mother announced she was going to Europe with a friend for three months. I was terrified at the prospect of having to do all of the cooking by myself. I didn't think I could handle it. As a savvy parent of five, though, my mom knew leaving was the only way I'd learn to do it myself. Left to my own devices (namely my Cuisinart) and with a little trial and error, I eventually figured things out on my own. I even developed some new recipes for our catering menu, like this Edamame Hummus recipe, which uses edamame (fresh green soybeans) instead of garbanzo beans. It's refreshing, bright and packed with soy protein. Served on a wonton chip, it'll be a huge hit at any party.

Serves 8 to 10 as an appetizer or snack
Preparation time: 20 minutes

8 oz (250 g, about 1½ cups) frozen shelled edamame (green soybeans)
2 tablespoons sesame seed paste or 4 tablespoons tahini
4 tablespoons water
½ teaspoon freshly grated lemon zest
3 tablespoons freshly squeezed lemon juice
1 clove garlic, smashed
¾ teaspoon kosher salt
½ teaspoon ground cumin
¼ teaspoon ground coriander
3 tablespoons extra-virgin olive oil

1 Cook the edamame according to package directions. Drain and rinse.
2 In a food processor, purée the edamame, sesame seed paste, water, lemon zest and juice, garlic, salt, cumin and coriander until smooth. With the motor running, slowly drizzle in the olive oil and mix until blended. Serve immediately with wonton chips, pita chips and cut up veggies.

Lettuce Wraps with Chicken

This recipe is remarkably easy and healthy, and is filled with lean protein. I remember when a glamorous and famous catering client of mine (sorry, can't name names!) asked for an appetizer menu that was 90% carb free. My mother looked at me like I had three heads when I told her. She didn't understand the low-carb craze. We put this fresh, light, flavorful and protein-packed appetizer on the menu and people went crazy for it. I also like to serve the filling in individual endive cups for cocktail parties. You can toss any leftover cooked meat with noodles for a delicious and simple lunch the next day. Ground turkey or pork may be substituted for the chicken.

Serves 3 to 4 as an appetizer or snack
Preparation time: 15 minutes
Cooking time: 5 minutes

1 lb (500 g) ground chicken
½ teaspoon salt
¼ teaspoon sugar
¼ teaspoon white pepper
2 teaspoons all-purpose cornstarch
1 small head iceberg or Bibb lettuce
2 teaspoons oil
½ cup (60 grams) coarsely chopped water chestnuts
2 large shallots, finely chopped
½ cup (125 ml) hoisin sauce, homemade (page 25) or store-bought
2 green onions (scallions), finely chopped

1 In a medium bowl, combine the chicken, salt, sugar, pepper and cornstarch. Cover and refrigerate for 20 minutes.

2 Carefully remove the lettuce leaves from the head. Take the six largest, nicest bowl-shaped leaves. Reserve the remaining leaves for another use. Trim the edges to form each leaf into a 4-inch (10-cm) bowl.

3 Heat the oil in a wok or skillet over medium-high heat. Add the chicken, water chestnuts and shallots and stir-fry for about 4 minutes, breaking up the chicken as it cooks. Remove from the heat.

4 Brush approximately 1 teaspoon hoisin sauce, or to taste, on each lettuce leaf. Place a scoop of filling in the center of each lettuce leaf. Garnish with green onion and serve with the remaining hoisin sauce.

Mu Shu Pork

This restaurant favorite, filled with tender slices of pork, egg, mushrooms and bamboo shoots stir-fried in a delicious sauce, hails from Northern China. My mother told me that Mu Shu means "flower blossoms" in Chinese, and the egg in the dish symbolizes yellow flower blossoms. There's an earthiness to this dish that traditionally comes from dried cloud ears, but I've substituted dried black mushrooms for ease and convenience. While Mu Shu is traditionally eaten in a steamed Chinese pancake, it's also delicious served over steaming-hot rice. Substitute chicken or beef for the pork if you wish.

Serves 8 as an appetizer or snack
Preparation time: 30 minutes + soaking
* and marinating time*
Cooking time: 7 to 8 minutes

1¼ lbs (600 g) boneless pork loin or leg, cut into thin strips
2 teaspoons all-purpose cornstarch, divided
1¼ teaspoons salt, divided
2 teaspoons soy sauce, divided
½ teaspoon sugar
½ teaspoon white pepper, plus a dash for the eggs
6 dried black mushrooms
2 tablespoons cold water
4 tablespoons oil, divided
1 egg, slightly beaten
1 clove garlic, minced
One 8.5-oz (260-g) can sliced bamboo shoots, drained and cut lengthwise into thin strips
½ cup (125 ml) chicken stock, either homemade (page 62) or store-bought
2 green onions (scallions), cut diagonally into 2-in (5-cm) pieces
Store-bought Chinese pancakes, steamed
Hoisin sauce, for serving (optional)

COOK'S NOTE
You can find Chinese pancakes at Asian markets. Warmed flour tortillas can be used as a substitute in a pinch.

1 Toss the pork together with 1 teaspoon of the cornstarch, 1 teaspoon of the salt, 1 teaspoon of the soy sauce, the sugar and ½ teaspoon of the white pepper in a medium bowl. Cover and refrigerate for 30 minutes.

2 Soak the mushrooms in hot water for 20 minutes or until soft. Rinse in warm water, drain and squeeze out excess moisture. Remove and discard stems; cut caps into thin strips.

3 Mix the remaining 1 teaspoon cornstarch with the water and the remaining 1 teaspoon soy sauce. Set aside.

4 Heat 2 tablespoons of the oil in a wok or skillet over medium heat. Combine the egg, the remaining ¼ teaspoon salt and a dash of white pepper. Pour the egg mixture into the wok or skillet, tilting to coat the bottom and form a thin pancake. Cook for 10 seconds or until firm, turning once. Remove the egg from the pan and cut into thin strips.

5 Heat the remaining 2 tablespoons oil in a wok or skillet over medium-high heat. Add the garlic and pork and stir-fry for about 2 minutes, until the meat is no longer pink. Add the mushrooms and bamboo shoots and stir-fry for 1 minute.

6 Stir in the chicken stock and cook, stirring, for 2 minutes. Add the cornstarch mixture and cook, stirring, for 10 seconds or until thickened. Add the green onions and reserved egg strips and stir-fry for another 30 seconds, then remove from heat.

7 To serve, spoon about 4 tablespoons of the pork mixture onto the center of each pancake. Fold two opposite sides over the filling, overlapping the edges about ½ inch (2.5 cm) in the center. Fold one unfolded edge over the folded sides to form a pocket. Serve with hoisin sauce if desired.

Salads

I n China, salads are a bit different than they are here in America. They tend to involve marinated vegetables, rather than lettuce and raw vegetables tossed with dressing like we eat here in the States. Like any dish on a Chinese dinner table, a salad is deliberately served to promote harmony during the meal: the yin of a cooling marinated cucumber salad balances out the yang of a spicy Sichuan dish.

I will be the first to cop to the fact that the salads in this chapter aren't salads you'd find in restaurants or homes in China. For instance, Chinese Chicken Salad (page 56). It's a purely American invention, but since it came onto the scene in the 1960s, its East-meets-West fusion of flavors and ingredients has made it one of the most popular salads of all time.

I had a lot of fun blending a variety of Chinese flavors to come up with my take on modern Chinese salads for this chapter. One of my favorites is the Napa Cabbage and Tofu Salad (page 59), because of the amazing textural combination enhanced by a sweet, spicy and tart dressing.

Another favorite is the Jade Shrimp Salad (page 57), made with gorgeous plump shrimp, mandarin oranges, spinach and pine nuts and tossed with a delicious vinaigrette. It wins rave reviews from all my friends because it's so fresh, healthy and satisfying.

I hope you try all of the salads in this chapter. I mean, who couldn't use a little harmony in their life?

Crab Mango Salad

Seafood is abundant is Guangzhou, China, where my family is from. I felt inspired to create this salad after a recent visit. Healthy, colorful and refreshing, this salad combines juicy ripe mango, lump crabmeat, cucumbers, red bell peppers and mixed baby greens in a bright lime-ginger dressing. I just served this at a ladies' lunch and everyone went wild for it. It's not fussy, yet it is luxurious—and that's how we all deserve to feel at times, right? Pair it with champagne and your friends will flip.

Serves 4 as part of a multi-course meal or for lunch
Preparation time: 25 minutes

DRESSING
4 tablespoons freshly squeezed lime juice
1 tablespoon honey
1 tablespoon soy sauce
1 teaspoon peeled and minced fresh ginger
½ teaspoon chili garlic sauce or sambal oelek
1 tablespoon dark sesame oil

12 oz (350 g) lump crabmeat, picked over for shells
1 cup (165 g) diced fresh mango
½ cup (50 g) peeled and seeded diced cucumber
½ cup (45 g) diced red bell pepper
4 cups (350 g) mixed baby greens

1 In a small bowl, whisk together all dressing ingredients except the sesame oil. Lastly, gradually whisk in the sesame oil until well blended.

2 In a large bowl, combine the crab, mango, cucumber, bell pepper and baby greens. Add the dressing and toss to combine. Serve immediately.

Ginger Shrimp and Sugar Snap Pea Salad

My friends who are ginger lovers adore this salad. It's packed with shrimp and fresh crunchy veggies like sugar snap peas, jicama, red bell pepper and English cucumber. It's then tossed in a flavorful soy-sesame dressing made, of course, with lots of ginger. My mom taught me a great trick for preparing ginger in advance: buy a pound (500 g) or so of fresh ginger, peel it, and cut it into medium chunks, then mince it in your food processor. Place the minced ginger in a large resealable food storage bag and pat it down so it's flat. Freeze the bag and then just snap off what you need for your recipes.

Serves 4 as part of a multi-course meal or for lunch
Preparation time: 25 to 30 minutes

DRESSING

3 tablespoons unseasoned rice vinegar or white vinegar
4 tablespoons finely chopped fresh coriander leaves (cilantro)
2 tablespoons soy sauce
1½ teaspoons peeled and minced fresh ginger
1 clove garlic, minced
½ teaspoon chili garlic sauce or sambal oelek
1 teaspoon toasted sesame seeds
1 teaspoon dark sesame oil

10 oz (330 g) sugar snap peas, trimmed, strings removed and cut in half on the diagonal
20 shelled and deveined medium-sized cooked shrimp
1 green onion (scallion), finely chopped
¼ cup (35 g) sliced water chestnuts
½ small jicama, peeled and cut into thin matchsticks
1 small red bell pepper, thinly sliced
½ English cucumber, cut into matchsticks

1 In a small bowl, whisk together all dressing ingredients except the sesame oil. Lastly, gradually whisk in the sesame oil until well blended.

2 Bring a medium saucepan of water to a boil. Add the sugar snap peas and blanch for 1 minute or until tender-crisp. Using a slotted spoon, transfer the peas to a bowl of ice water to chill, then drain.

3 Combine the sugar snap peas, shrimp, green onion, water chestnuts, jicama, red bell pepper and cucumber. Add the dressing and toss to combine. Serve immediately.

Chinese Chicken Salad

Legend has it that Chinese Chicken Salad was invented in Los Angeles in the sixties, when Madame Wu served it to Cary Grant at her eponymous restaurant in Santa Monica. He flipped for it, and the rest is history. Chinese Chicken Salads in the U.S. really run the gamut. The one I'm sharing with you is light, healthy and filled with a fantastic variety of textures, from the red cabbage (loaded with vitamins, nutrients and anti-oxidants, by the way) and carrots to the sliced almonds and crunchy wonton chips, all tossed in a yummy ginger-sesame dressing.

Serves 4 as part of a multi-course meal or for lunch
Preparation time: 25 minutes

DRESSING
⅓ cup (80 ml) unseasoned rice wine vinegar or white
    vinegar
1 clove garlic, minced
1 teaspoon peeled and minced fresh ginger
2 tablespoons brown sugar
1½ teaspoons chili garlic sauce or sambal oelek
2 tablespoons extra-virgin olive or canola oil
1 teaspoon dark sesame oil

6 cups (300 g) romaine lettuce, torn into bite-sized pieces
¼ head red cabbage, shredded
1 large carrot, shredded
2 green onions (scallions), green and white parts, finely
    chopped
½ cup (50 g) sliced almonds, plus more for garnish
One 11-oz (340-g) can mandarin oranges in water, drained
2 cups (300 g) shredded store-bought rotisserie chicken
    meat (or grilled chicken breast slices)
½ cup (20 g) fried wonton strips, plus more for garnish
2 tablespoons toasted sesame seeds, plus more for garnish

1 Make the dressing: In a small bowl, whisk together the vinegar, garlic, ginger, brown sugar and chili garlic sauce. Gradually whisk in the olive or canola oil and the sesame oil.

2 In a large bowl, combine the romaine lettuce, red cabbage, carrot, green onion, sliced almonds, mandarin oranges, shredded chicken, wonton strips and toasted sesame seeds. Pour dressing over and toss to combine. Garnish with additional sliced almonds, wonton strips and sesame seeds. Serve immediately.

Jade Shrimp Salad

I love this fresh, nutty and satisfying, tender shrimp-laden salad so much, I buy huge bags of spinach so I can get my fix anytime. Because this salad is a great source of folic acid, my husband made it for me all the time when I was pregnant with the twins. The tart-sweet flavors from the orange marmalade marry perfectly with the ginger-soy dressing sweetened with a bit of honey. I'm not sure how Jade Shrimp got its name, but my mother said she was told as a little girl it was because cooked shrimp resembles the ethereal color of white jade.

Serves 4 as part of a multi-course meal or for lunch
Preparation time: 20 Minutes

VINAIGRETTE
2 tablespoons plus 2 teaspoons orange marmalade
⅛ teaspoon ground red pepper (cayenne)
½ teaspoon peeled and minced fresh ginger
⅛ teaspoon garlic powder
2 tablespoons rice vinegar or white vinegar
1 tablespoon soy sauce
1 tablespoon honey
⅓ cup (80 ml) canola or extra-virgin olive oil
1 tablespoon plus 1½ teaspoons dark sesame oil

16 cooked medium-sized shrimp, shelled and deveined
2 green onions (scallions), white and green parts, finely
    chopped
4 tablespoons canned chopped water chestnuts, rinsed
    and drained
4 tablespoons toasted pine nuts, plus more for garnish
One 11-oz (340-g) can mandarin oranges, drained
½ cup (75 g) cucumber, cut into matchsticks
4 cups (120 g) baby spinach for four salad plates

1 Make the vinaigrette: Place all dressing ingredients except the olive or canola oil and sesame oil in a blender or food processor. Blend for approximately 30 seconds. With the motor still running, slowly pour in the oils and blend for another 15 seconds.

2 In a large bowl, combine the shrimp, green onions, water chestnuts, pine nuts, mandarin oranges and cucumber. Pour the dressing over and toss to combine.

3 Divide spinach evenly among four plates. Place salad mixture on top of spinach and garnish with more pine nuts. Serve immediately.

Soy Ginger Edamame Salad

Our friends Rich and Adam had just moved into a fabulous new house and had been unpacking all week. When we offered to bring over dinner, we knew they were longing for something other than takeout that was light, healthy and nutritious. This recipe was a great choice for that hot summer day! It couldn't be easier to make; it's just three main ingredients—edamame, red bell pepper, and jicama—accompanied by green onion, pine nuts and fresh coriander leaves, all tossed in a simple, bright dressing. This recipe is proof that sometimes simple can be sublime.

Serves 4 as part of a multi-course meal or for lunch
Preparation time: 20 minutes

DRESSING

4 tablespoons soy sauce
2 tablespoons freshly squeezed lime juice
1 tablespoon plus 1 teaspoon unseasoned rice vinegar or white vinegar
1 teaspoon peeled and minced fresh ginger
1 tablespoon plus 1 teaspoon olive or canola oil
1 teaspoon dark sesame oil
Salt and pepper, to taste

2½ cups (375 g) shelled frozen edamame (green soybeans)
½ cup (85 g) chopped red bell pepper
½ cup (60 g) jicama, peeled and cubed
4 tablespoons green onion (scallion), finely chopped (green and white parts), plus more for garnish
2 tablespoons toasted pine nuts
4 tablespoons finely chopped fresh coriander leaves (cilantro)

1 Make the dressing: In a small bowl, whisk together the soy sauce, lime juice, vinegar and ginger. Gradually whisk in the olive or canola oil and sesame oil until well blended. Add salt and pepper to taste.

2 Cook the edamame according to package directions, then rinse with cold water and drain.

3 In a large bowl, combine the edamame, red bell pepper, jicama, green onion, pine nuts and fresh coriander leaves. Pour the dressing over and toss. Garnish with additional green onion and serve immediately.

Napa Cabbage and Tofu Salad

Napa cabbage, also known as Chinese cabbage, originated in Beijing; my mother always told me it was a symbol of prosperity. It has an oblong shape (similar to a gold ingot, which may be what connects it to prosperity) and thick, crisp stems with frilly yellow-green leaves. It tastes a bit sweeter than other kinds of green cabbage, and it's great in salads as well as cooked foods. I pair Napa cabbage with red cabbage in this recipe, along with the slivered almonds and Asian pear, for a colorful medley of textures. Tossed with a bright and refreshing dressing of ginger, garlic, orange juice and other Chinese flavors, this salad is a hit with all of my friends—vegetarian or otherwise!

Serves 4 as part of a multi-course meal or for lunch
Preparation time: 25 to 30 minutes

DRESSING
1 teaspoon Asian chili sauce such as Sriracha
2 teaspoons peeled and minced fresh ginger
1 clove garlic, minced
2 tablespoons freshly squeezed orange juice
1½ tablespoons soy sauce
1 tablespoon olive or canola oil
1 tablespoon dark sesame oil

12 oz (375 g) extra-firm tofu, drained, patted dry and diced
3 cups (300 g) Napa cabbage, cut into shreds
1 cup (100 g) red cabbage, cut into shreds
1 small carrot, cut into matchsticks
1 Asian pear, cut into matchsticks and tossed with juice of ½ lemon
4 tablespoons sliced or slivered almonds, toasted

1 Make the dressing: In a small bowl, whisk together the chili sauce, ginger, garlic, orange juice and soy sauce. Gradually whisk in the olive or canola oil and sesame oil until well blended.

2 In a large bowl, combine the tofu, Napa cabbage, red cabbage, carrot, pear and almonds together. Add the dressing and toss to combine. Serve immediately.

COOK'S NOTE
For added protein, add 1 cup (75 g) shredded cooked chicken or chopped shrimp.

Soups

———

Soups have played an important role in Chinese cuisine for centuries. From the decadent shark's-fin soup served to emperors at dynastic banquets to the simple clear broths with a few vegetables enjoyed by villagers, soups are revered in China for their healing and soothing qualities. You'll always find soup on a Chinese dinner table instead of water, as the Chinese believe it's unhealthy to drink cool beverages. Soups are enjoyed as a way to hydrate the body, and are sipped between mouthfuls of other dishes.

Luckily for all of us, with so much attention paid toward soup in Chinese history, we have a bounty of delicious, healthy and easy soups to choose from that can be made with everyday ingredients. For this section, I've put together a selection of the soups my mother made for us growing up, like hearty Beef with Rice Stick Noodle Soup (page 63) and light and healthy Tofu Tomato Soup (page 68), as well as all-time Chinese restaurant favorites like sweet and soothing Velvet Chicken Corn Soup (page 67) and the Sichuan classic Hot-and-Sour Soup (page 65).

I've also included recipes for basic stocks. A good chicken stock (page 62) simmered with ginger is the foundation of Cantonese cooking, resulting in sumptuous soups and velvety stir-fry gravies. Of course, it's absolutely fine to use store-bought stock in your soups, but if you have some time on a lazy Sunday afternoon, it's totally worth it to boil up a big pot of homemade stock. Try it and you'll see what I mean.

Basic Chicken Stock

My mother taught me that good chicken stock is the backbone of Chinese cooking. It adds richness to the gravies in stir-fries and gives depth and flavor to soups. The key is to boil the chicken bones briefly first, then rinse them and return them to the pot. Chicken stock knows it wouldn't amount to anything without its frisky sidekick ginger. Paired together in this stock, they'll give all of your favorite recipes greater savor and richness.

Makes 2 quarts (1.75 liters)
Preparation time: 5 minutes
Cooking time: 2½ hours + cooling time

3 lbs (1.5 kg) bony chicken pieces
Four ¼-in (6-mm) thick slices fresh ginger
2 quarts (1.75 liters) water

1 Fill a stock pot two-thirds full with water and bring to a boil. Add chicken bones and boil for 3 minutes. Pour out the water and rinse the bones.

2 Return the bones to the stock pot. Add the ginger and the 2 quarts (1.75 liters) water. Cover and bring to a boil, then reduce the heat to medium low. Skim the fat and foam off the top. Simmer uncovered for 2 hours, continue to skim the foam off the top frequently. Strain and cool before storing in the refrigerator.

COOK'S NOTE
Freeze 2-tablespoon portions of stock in ice cube trays. It's easy to pop out a cube or two whenever you're stir-frying!

Basic Fish Stock

Fish stock, used for seafood soups and sauces, requires a lot less time to simmer than chicken stock. Stir-frying the bones briefly eliminates the fish smell and flavor from this stock. The result is soups and sauces that taste clean and bright.

Makes 2 quarts (1.75 liters)
Preparation time: 5 minutes
Cooking time: 50 minutes + cooling time

2 tablespoons oil
2 lbs (1 kg) fish bones and head (gills removed)
1 leek, white part only, cleaned and cut into ½-in (1.25-cm) slices across the stalk
2 shallots, chopped
2 teaspoons finely chopped fresh ginger
2 cloves garlic, minced
2 quarts (1.75 liters) water
1 teaspoon salt

1 Heat the oil in a stockpot over medium-high heat. Add the fish bones and stir-fry for about 3 minutes, or until pink. Add the leek, shallots, ginger, garlic, and water. Cover and bring to a boil.

2 Reduce the heat to medium-low and simmer uncovered for 15 minutes. Skim the fat and foam off the top. Simmer uncovered for 20 minutes more, continuing to skim the foam off the top often. Strain and cool before storing in the refrigerator.

Beef with Rice Stick Noodle Soup

My kids are always on the run, so when I need to entice them into sitting down for five minutes to eat, it has to be something that's yummy first and nutritious second. In my house, noodles always do the trick. Whenever I make this soup, they sit down for an average of ten (not five) minutes, and instead of talking, all I hear is slurping. I know the beef in this soup will give them energy for the rest of the day. This rich, soothing and hearty soup is perfect on a chilly day or anytime you want a light, yet filling lunch.

Serves 2 to 3 as part of a multi-course meal or
    for lunch
Preparation time: 10 minutes
Cooking time: 20 minutes

5 oz (150 g) dried rice stick noodles
¼ teaspoon salt
⅛ teaspoon white pepper
1 teaspoon peeled and minced fresh ginger
½ teaspoon all-purpose cornstarch
4 cups (1 liter) beef or chicken stock, homemade
    (opposite) or store-bought
4 oz (100 g) beef sirloin or flank steak, cut across the
    grain into thin slices
1 tablespoon fish sauce
½ teaspoon dark sesame oil
2 tablespoons finely chopped fresh coriander (cilantro)
    leaves

1 Bring a large pot of water to a boil. Remove from the heat. Immerse the noodles in the hot water and let stand, stirring occasionally, for 10 minutes or until the noodles are soft, yet firm. Drain well and rinse with cool water.

2 Combine the salt, pepper, ginger and cornstarch in a small bowl. Set aside.

3 Bring 8 cups (1.75 liters) water to a boil in a large pot. Add the reserved noodles and boil for 30 seconds. Drain well and place the noodles in serving bowls.

4 Bring the stock to a boil in a large pot. Stir in the beef, fish sauce, and sesame oil. Return to boiling and add the cornstarch mixture and cook for 20 seconds while stirring. Turn off the heat. Pour the beef soup over the noodles and garnish with the cilantro leaves.

Egg Drop Soup

This humble and tasty soup, known for its silky egg finish, is a Chinese classic, even though it's among the simplest soups in the world to make. My mother told me its Chinese name means "Egg Flowers Soup." She ate this soup as a little girl growing up; their family cook would serve a huge bowl of it for the family meal, made with homemade chicken stock, fresh eggs from the family farm and green onions from their garden. The only trick is to be sure the stock is at a full, rolling boil as you stir in the beaten eggs. This ensures that the soup's signature thin strands of cooked egg float throughout.

Serves 4 as part of a multi-course meal
Preparation time: 5 minutes
Cooking time: 10 minutes

4 cups (1 liter) chicken stock, homemade (page 62) or store-bought
1 teaspoon salt
Dash of white pepper
1 green onion (scallion), white and green parts, finely chopped
2 large eggs, slightly beaten

1 Bring the chicken stock, salt and white pepper to a rolling boil in a medium pot.

2 Stir the green onion into the eggs. Pour the egg mixture slowly into the stock, stirring constantly with fork, until it forms into strands. Remove from the heat and serve immediately.

COOK'S NOTE
The stock must come be at a rolling boil, or the egg won't form into strands when it is added.

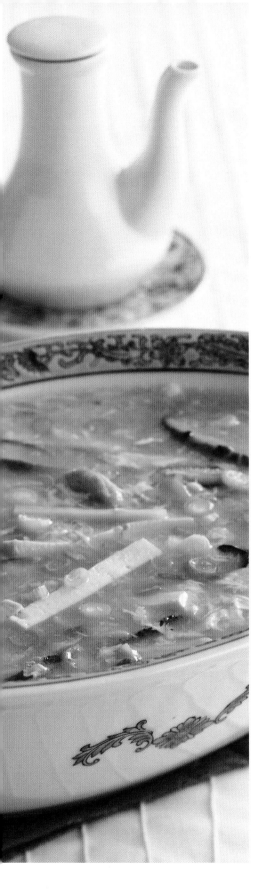

Hot-and-Sour Soup

This Sichuan classic is a staple at Chinese restaurants all over China and here in the U.S. Made with tender strips of pork, soy sauce, vinegar and hot sauce, it's the perfect balance of sour and spicy. It also supposedly aids in digestion, especially when you're also enjoying something crispy like sweet-and-sour chicken as part of the meal. When my brother Billy came home from college for summer break, he'd often heat up a bowl of Hot-and-Sour Soup for breakfast, which I always thought was bizarre. Years later, he shared his secret with me after spending a night out on the town during *my* college break—it's an awesome hangover remedy!

Serves 4 as part of a multi-course meal
Preparation time: 10 minutes + soaking and marinating time
Cooking time: 8 minutes

6 medium black mushrooms
4 oz (100 g) boneless pork loin, cut into thin strips
2½ teaspoons all-purpose cornstarch, divided
1½ teaspoons salt, divided
½ teaspoon plus 1 tablespoon soy sauce, divided
4 cups (1 liter) chicken stock, homemade (page 62) or store-bought
3 tablespoons white vinegar
4 oz (100 g) shredded canned bamboo shoots
5 oz (150 g) medium-firm tofu, drained, patted dry and cut into thin strips
2 tablespoons cold water
¼ teaspoon white pepper
2 large eggs, slightly beaten
2 tablespoons finely chopped green onion (scallion), white and green parts
2 teaspoons Asian chili sauce, such as Sriracha
½ teaspoon dark sesame oil

1 Soak the black mushrooms in hot water for 20 minutes, or until soft. Discard soaking water. Cut off the stems and discard. Cut the mushroom caps into ½-inch (1.25-cm) pieces.

2 In a medium bowl, toss the pork with ½ teaspoon of the cornstarch, ½ teaspoon of the salt and ½ teaspoon of the soy sauce. Cover and refrigerate for 15 minutes.

3 Bring the chicken stock, vinegar, remaining 1 tablespoon soy sauce and remaining 1 teaspoon salt to a boil in a medium pot. Add the bamboo shoots, soaked mushrooms, pork and tofu. Bring back to a boil, then reduce heat and simmer for 5 minutes, covered.

4 Mix the remaining 2 tablespoons cornstarch with the cold water and white pepper. Stir into the soup and bring to a rolling boil. Slowly pour the egg into the soup, stirring constantly with a fork until the egg forms strands. Add the green onions, chili sauce and sesame oil and stir for 30 seconds. Serve immediately.

Chicken, Bok Choy and Clam Soup

Whenever my siblings or I felt lethargic, my mom would whip up a pot of this soup. Beef was a luxury for us growing up, but she knew that clams were loaded with iron and could fortify us with the energy required to be the "mathletes" we (at least everyone but me) were destined to become. This is a delicious soup that lets the flavor of the clams shine through, with just a bit of red wine, garlic and ginger to flavor the delicate broth, dotted with crisp and tender slices of bok choy.

Serves 4 as part of a multi-course meal
Preparation time: 15 minutes
Cooking time: 15 minutes

16 clams
5 cups (1.25 liters) chicken stock, homemade (page 62) or
    store-bought
Two ¼-in (6-mm) thick slices fresh ginger
2 cups (150 g) sliced bok choy
1 tablespoon oil
2 cloves garlic, minced
4 tablespoons red wine
4 oz (100 g) cooked chicken breast, thinly sliced
1 green onion (scallion), finely chopped (white and green
    parts)

1 Brush the clams very well under cold running water and drain. Set aside.

2 Bring the stock and ginger to a boil in a medium saucepan. Add the bok choy and cook for 1 minute. Reduce heat and let simmer.

3 While the stock is simmering, heat the oil in a wok or skillet over medium-high heat. Add the garlic and clams and stir-fry for 30 seconds. Add the red wine, cover and cook for 2 minutes, or until the clams open (discard any clams that stay closed). Remove the clams and add the clam cooking liquid to the simmering chicken broth. Add the sliced chicken breast and bring the broth back to a boil.

4 Remove from heat and pour soup into 4 serving bowls. Place 4 clams on top of each soup bowl and garnish with green onion.

COOK'S NOTE
It's best to purchase clams right before cooking, but if you must buy them in advance, keep them moist on ice in the fridge. If any are open, tap the shell. If they don't close tightly, discard them.

Velvet Chicken Corn Soup

This gentle, soothing soup is flecked with tiny, tender bits of chicken, strands of egg white and juicy kernels of corn. The velvetiness of the eggs makes it seem like it has cream in it, but it's completely dairy-free. My mother fed us a lot of soups when we were babies because of the high calcium content in her homemade chicken stock. I have a fond memory of her giving small spoonfuls of this soup to my son Dylan when he was just a year old. He started kicking his feet because it was so delicious, and from that day on he became known in our household as the "Corn Master."

Serves 4 as part of a multi-course meal
Preparation time: 10 minutes
Cooking time: 10 minutes

4 oz (100 g) ground chicken
2 egg whites
½ teaspoon dark sesame oil
¼ teaspoon salt
⅛ teaspoon white pepper
1 teaspoon peeled and minced fresh ginger
2 tablespoons all-purpose cornstarch
4 cups (1 liter) chicken stock, homemade (page 62) or store-bought
¾ cup (130 g) fresh or thawed frozen corn kernels
1 tablespoon chopped green onion (scallion), white and green parts or chopped fresh coriander, for garnish

1 In a large bowl, combine the chicken, egg whites, sesame oil, salt, pepper, ginger and cornstarch.

2 Bring the chicken stock to a boil in a medium pot. Slowly add the chicken mixture and the corn to the broth, stirring constantly, and bring back to a boil. Turn off the heat. Garnish with the green onion or coriander to serve.

Tofu Tomato Soup

We call my husband Matthew the "Tomato Whisperer" because he grows the most amazing tomatoes. They're coveted by our neighbors far and wide. When my mother was living with us, she was constantly coming up with new ways to cook with her son-in-law's bounty. One of my favorites is this simple and delicious Tofu Tomato Soup. Bursting with fresh tomatoes, it's a healthy, protein-packed soup with an earthy umami punch from the black mushrooms.

Serves 4 as part of a multi-course meal
Preparation time: 10 minutes + soaking time
Cooking time: 18 minutes

3 dried black mushrooms
2 large eggs
½ teaspoon salt
Pinch white pepper
2 teaspoons all-purpose cornstarch
2 teaspoons water
4 cups (1 liter) chicken stock, homemade (page 62) or store-bought
10 oz (330 g) firm tofu, drained, patted dry and diced
1 large tomato, diced
½ cup (70 g) fresh or frozen peas

1 Soak the black mushrooms in hot water for 20 minutes, or until soft. Discard soaking water. Cut off the stems and discard. Cut the mushroom caps into ½-inch (1.25-cm) pieces.

2 In a medium bowl, whisk together the eggs, salt and pepper.

3 In a small bowl, mix the cornstarch with the water.

4 Combine the mushrooms and the chicken stock in a medium pot and bring to a boil. Cook for 5 minutes, then add the tofu, tomato and peas and return to a boil.

5 Lower the heat, stir in the cornstarch mixture and return to high heat. When the soup comes to a rolling boil, pour in a spoonful of the egg mixture, stirring in a circular motion. When the egg forms into thin strands, continue to add spoonfuls of the egg to the boiling soup, stirring constantly with a fork until all the egg has formed strands, about 30 seconds. Serve immediately.

Spicy Pork Noodle Soup

The Sichuan province of China is renowned for its spicy dishes because of the abundance of hot chili peppers in the region. This soup is reminiscent of many of the fiery dishes my mom and I tasted on our trips together to Sichuan. You can adjust the heat level by adding more or less red chili pepper. Don't deseed the peppers if you were Sichuan in another life—the seeds pack the most punch! I always keep a few packages of rice noodles on hand so I can whip up this deliciously hot soup anytime.

Serves 4 as part of a multi-course meal
Preparation time: 15 minutes + marinating time
Cooking time: 15 minutes

6 oz (175 g) dried rice stick noodles
¼ teaspoon salt
¼ teaspoon white pepper
1 teaspoon all-purpose cornstarch
4 oz (100 g) pork tenderloin, cut into thin strips
2 teaspoons oil
2 tablespoons chili paste, homemade (page 25) or store-bought
1 clove garlic, minced
1 fresh hot red chili pepper, thinly sliced (deseeded if you prefer less heat)
4 cups (1 liter) chicken stock, homemade (page 62) or store-bought
2 green onions (scallions), white and green parts, finely chopped, some reserved
   for garnish

1 Bring a large pot of water to a boil, then remove from the heat. Immerse the noodles and soak, stirring occasionally, until they are soft, yet firm, about 10 minutes. Drain well and rinse with cool water.

2 In a medium bowl, mix the salt, pepper and cornstarch. Add the pork and toss to combine. Cover and refrigerate for 20 minutes.

3 Heat the oil in a medium pot over medium-high heat. Add the chili paste, garlic and chili pepper and stir-fry for 1 minute. Add the chicken stock and bring to a boil.

4 Add the pork and the rice noodles. Stir to separate the pork pieces. Return to boiling water again for 20 seconds and turn off the heat. Add the green onions and stir to combine. Serve immediately and garnish with more green onions.

COOK'S NOTE
If you can't find chili paste, you can substitute chili garlic sauce or an Asian hot sauce like Sriracha. Just add it at the same time as the rice noodles.

Wor Wonton Soup

Wor in Chinese means "everything," so basically anything and everything can go into this soup. My mother and father never wasted food. In fact, we couldn't leave the table growing up unless we ate every single solitary grain of rice in our bowls. Needless to say, we ate a lot of this soup, because it's perfect for leftovers. My mom would add morsels of delicious barbecued pork or slices of roast duck from our dinner the night before into this rich and flavorful broth. This recipe calls for cooked chicken, barbecued pork and shrimp, but feel free to experiment with whatever meat, seafood or veggies you may have on hand.

Serves 4 as part of a multi-course meal
Preparation time: 30 minutes
Cooking time: 12 minutes

WONTON FILLING
8 shelled and deveined medium-sized raw shrimp
1 oz (25 g) ground pork or chicken
2 canned water chestnuts, finely chopped
1 green onion (scallion), finely chopped
½ teaspoon all-purpose cornstarch
¼ teaspoon salt
⅛ teaspoon toasted sesame oil
Dash of white pepper

12 wonton wrappers
1 egg white, slightly beaten
4 snow peas, trimmed and tips removed, halved lengthwise
3 cups (750 ml) water
2 cups (500 ml) chicken stock, homemade (page 62) or
    store-bought
4 white button mushrooms, stemmed and thinly sliced
4 medium shrimp, peeled and deveined
4 slices barbecued pork, homemade (page 41) or store-
    bought
¼ cup (35 g) shredded cooked chicken breast
Two ¼-in (6-mm) thick slices fresh ginger
4 sliced canned bamboo shoots
½ teaspoon salt
Dash of white pepper
1 tablespoon finely chopped green onion (scallion),
    white and green parts
⅛ teaspoon dark sesame oil

1 This recipe calls for a total of 12 medium shrimp. Follow the directions for "Eliminating Shrimp's 'Fishy' Taste" on page 20. (This step is optional.)

2 Make the wonton filling: Finely chop 8 of the shrimp. Combine with all other filling ingredients in a medium bowl and mix to blend.

3 Lay a wonton wrapper on a clean work surface (cover remaining wrappers with plastic wrap or a damp towel to keep them pliable). Place ½ teaspoon of the wonton filling in the center. Fold one corner of the wonton wrapper over the filling to form a triangle. Brush the right corner of the triangle with egg white. Bring the right and left corners together below the filling and pinch together to seal. Repeat with remaining wonton wrappers.

4 Fill a medium pot ⅔ full with water and heat to boiling. Add the wontons and return to a boil, then reduce heat to medium-low and simmer uncovered for 2 minutes. Remove wontons with a slotted spoon and place in ice water to keep them from sticking together.

5 Blanch the snow peas in boiling water until tender, about 1 minute. Using a slotted spoon, transfer the snow peas to an ice water bath to cool, then drain and set aside.

6 Bring the 3 cups (750 ml) water, chicken stock and mushrooms to a boil in a medium-sized pot. Add the 4 remaining shrimp and cook for 3 minutes. Drain the wontons and stir them into the stock. Add the barbecued pork slices, shredded chicken, ginger slices, bamboo shoots, salt and pepper. Return to a boil, then reduce the heat to medium low. Simmer for 2 minutes. Add the snow peas, green onions and sesame oil. Ladle into bowls and serve immediately.

Vegetable, Egg and Ramen Soup

Packaged ramen soup is one of my guilty pleasures (another is binge-watching *Scandal*). I eat it about once a year, and it brings back memories of cramming for finals at Boston University, but then I feel yucky from all the sodium. For this recipe, I wanted to create a healthy, home-style version of ramen soup in a nutrient-rich broth brimming with the flavors of onion, garlic and black pepper. It's such a flavorful soup that my kids don't seem to mind gobbling up the carrots, spinach and mushrooms in this soup.

Serves 4 as part of a multi-course meal
Preparation time: 15 minutes
Cooking time: 20 minutes

8 oz (250 g) dried Chinese egg noodles, or 4 oz (115 g) fresh egg noodles
6 cups (1.5 liters) chicken stock, homemade (page 62) or store-bought
2 cups (500 ml) water
Four ¼-in (6-mm) thick slices fresh ginger
½ teaspoon dark sesame oil
2 teaspoons salt
1 tablespoon onion powder
1 tablespoon garlic powder
½ teaspoon freshly ground black pepper
1 cup (150 g) thinly sliced carrots, cut on the diagonal
2 large eggs, beaten
1 cup (70 g) sliced white button mushrooms
4 cups (120 g) fresh baby spinach leaves
4 tablespoons finely chopped green onion (scallion), white and green
    parts, for garnish
Soy sauce, for serving

1 Prepare the noodles according to package directions. Drain and set aside.

2 Bring the chicken stock and water to a boil. Add the ginger slices, sesame oil, salt, onion powder, garlic powder, pepper and carrots and cook for 3 minutes.

3 Pour in a spoonful of the egg mixture, stirring in a circular motion. When shreds have formed, continue to add spoonfuls of the egg mixture to the boiling soup, stirring constantly with a fork until all the egg mixture forms shreds, about 30 seconds.

4 Add the noodles, mushrooms and spinach and simmer for 1 minute. Garnish with green onion and serve immediately with soy sauce.

Poultry

My friend Maureen sent me this text the other day: "Help! I've run out of chicken ideas. Kids are starving!" I can't tell you the number of friends who struggle with finding new ways to cook something interesting with chicken. Chicken is something that almost everyone likes, so why not put a Chinese spin on it? In this chapter, I've put together simple and delicious chicken recipes that both your friends and family will love.

Chickens are abundant in China, so it's no wonder that many popular Chinese dishes are made with chicken. Chicken's subtle flavor also marries well with the seasonings and spices in Chinese cuisine. During my family's humble beginnings in Minnesota, my mother often made chicken because she could feed our large extended family easily and economically. By using the freshest ingredients (she grew her own bok choy in our garden) and time-honored techniques, she was able to turn a simple chicken breast into a succulent gourmet Chinese meal. Even though we didn't have a lot of money, she always made us feel rich sitting at our dinner table.

I've included simple and healthy stir-fries that are great for busy weeknights, as well as the all-time favorites; General Tso's Chicken (page 78) and Orange Chicken (page 74).

The *piece de resistance* is my mother's famous Lemon Chicken recipe (page 77). Crispy, tender and topped with an intoxicating lemony glaze, her Lemon Chicken is definitely worth clucking about.

Orange Chicken

If you love orange chicken at restaurants, you'll be thrilled to master this dish at home, which has a much lighter batter and sauce compared to the thick, heavy affair you sometimes find at Chinese restaurants and the mall food court. Tender pieces of chicken are marinated, lightly fried in a simple batter and then quickly fried again (this is my mother's secret deep-frying technique, which I like to call the "Chinese Two-Step"). The sauce is sweet, sour and slightly spicy, and when poured over the most crispety-crunchety chicken you'll ever have, the result is mouthwatering, crispy, juicy and delicious!

Serves 4 to 6 as part of a multi-course meal
Preparation time: 20 minutes + marinating time
Cooking time: 25 minutes

MARINADE
1 large egg, slightly beaten
½ tablespoon all-purpose cornstarch
1 teaspoon soy sauce
½ teaspoon salt
Dash of white pepper

ORANGE SAUCE
2 tablespoons all-purpose cornstarch
2 tablespoons water
¾ cups (150 g) sugar
½ cup (125 ml) chicken stock, homemade (page 62) or store-bought
2 tablespoons orange juice concentrate
6 tablespoons unseasoned rice vinegar or white vinegar
2 teaspoons oil
2 teaspoons dark soy sauce
¼ teaspoon salt
1 clove garlic, minced
¼ teaspoon crushed red pepper
¼ teaspoon orange zest

BATTER
¼ cup (30 g) all-purpose flour
4 tablespoons water
2 tablespoons all-purpose cornstarch
2 teaspoons oil
¼ teaspoon salt
¼ teaspoon baking soda

1 lb (500 g) boneless, skinless or breast or thigh, cut into 1-in (2.5-cm) cubes
Oil for frying
Orange slices for garnish

1 Make the marinade: In a medium bowl, combine the egg, cornstarch, soy sauce, salt and pepper. Add the chicken pieces and toss to coat. Cover and refrigerate for 20 minutes. Remove the chicken, reserving the marinade.

2 Make the orange sauce: Combine the cornstarch and water in a small bowl and set aside. Combine the sugar, chicken stock, orange juice concentrate, vinegar, oil, soy sauce, salt, garlic, crushed red pepper and orange zest in a medium saucepan and bring to a boil. Add the cornstarch mixture to the sauce and cook, stirring continuously, until the sauce thickens, about 10 seconds. Remove from heat and set aside.

3 Make the batter: Combine all batter ingredients and mix to blend. Stir in the chicken pieces and reserved marinade into the batter until the meat is well coated.

4 In a wok or skillet, heat 2 to 3 inches (5 to 7.5 cm) of frying oil to 350°F (175°C). Fry about 15 chicken pieces at a time, turning frequently, until lightly browned, about 3 minutes. Drain on a paper-towel-lined sheet pan.

5 Increase oil temperature to 375°F (190°C). Re-fry all the chicken pieces at once for 1 minute. Drain on a paper-towel-lined sheet pan. Transfer the chicken pieces to a serving platter.

6 Reheat the sauce over medium-high heat and pour over the chicken. Garnish with orange slices and serve immediately with steaming-hot rice.

COOK'S NOTE
Leave out the crushed red pepper if you're cooking for young children.

Bring the sauce ingredients to a boil before adding the cornstarch mixture to the sauce.

Stir reserved marinade into the batter.

Add the marinated chicken pieces to the batter and combine until coated evenly.

Fry about 15 battered chicken pieces at a time in a wok or skillet.

Reheat the sauce over medium-high heat and pour over the chicken.

Cashew Chicken

Our friends Eleni and Joe, and their son Michael, came to spend the Fourth of July at our lake home. Michael is only six, but he eats like he's sixteen (nothing makes a Chinese cook happier!), so I decided to make a giant batch of Cashew Chicken. Everyone loved it, and Michael ate his fill! Loaded with tender chicken and crunchy sweet cashews, this dish is a classic Cantonese favorite. The bit of Chinese rice wine adds wonderful depth; if you can't find Chinese rice wine, then dry sherry is a fine substitute.

Serves 4 to 6 as part of a multi-course meal
Preparation time: 20 minutes + marinating time
Cooking time: 10 minutes

12 oz (350 g) boneless, skinless chicken breast or thigh, cut into small cubes
3 teaspoons all-purpose cornstarch, divided
½ teaspoon salt
Dash of white pepper
2 tablespoons hoisin sauce, homemade (page 25) or store-bought
1 teaspoon Chinese rice wine or sherry
1 teaspoon sugar
1 teaspoon soy sauce
1 teaspoon dark sesame oil
2 teaspoons water
2 tablespoons oil, divided
1 clove garlic, minced
1 teaspoon peeled and minced fresh ginger
1 small onion, cut into ½-in (1.25-cm) cubes
1 small red bell pepper, cut into ½-in (1.25-cm) cubes
½ cup (75 g) roasted cashews
½ cup (125 ml) chicken stock, homemade (page 62) or store-bought
Green onion (scallion), finely chopped, for garnish

1 Toss the chicken with 1 teaspoon of the cornstarch, the salt, and the pepper in a small bowl. Cover and refrigerate for 10 minutes.

2 In a small bowl, mix together the remaining 2 teaspoons of cornstarch with the hoisin sauce, rice wine or sherry, sugar, soy sauce, sesame oil and water. Set aside.

3 Heat 1 tablespoon of the oil in a wok or skillet over medium-high heat. Add the chicken and stir-fry until the meat turns white, about 2 minutes. Remove the chicken from the pan and set aside.

4 Wash and thoroughly dry the wok, then heat the remaining 1 tablespoon oil over medium-high heat. When hot, stir in the garlic, ginger and onion and stir-fry until fragrant, about 1 minute. Add the reserved chicken and bell pepper and stir-fry for 1 minute. Pour in the chicken stock and let come to a boil. Add the cornstarch mixture and stir-fry until the sauce has thickened, about 2 minutes. Add the cashews and stir-fry 1 minute more.

5 Dish out and garnish with green onion. Serve immediately with jasmine rice.

Lemon Chicken

Pucker up, folks, because this lemon chicken is out of this world! This was my mother's signature dish, and she served tons (I mean, literally tons) of it to her catering clients and at her restaurants. When fried, the batter becomes incredibly light and crispy. The sauce is bright, fresh and (of course) super-duper lemony, making for the perfect balance of sweet and tart. This is a great dish to serve at a dinner party, because you can keep the chicken warm in the oven while you're having cocktails, and then simply heat up the sauce and pour it over the chicken just before serving dinner.

Serves 4 to 6 as part of a multi-course meal
Preparation time: 15 minutes + marinating time
cooking time: 20 minutes

1 lb (500 g) boneless, skinless chicken breast
1 large egg
2 teaspoons plus 2 tablespoons all-purpose
    cornstarch, divided
1¼ teaspoons salt, divided
¼ teaspoon white pepper
1 teaspoon peeled and minced fresh ginger

LEMON SAUCE
½ tablespoon all-purpose cornstarch
½ tablespoon cold water
4 tablespoons chicken stock, homemade (page 62)
    or store-bought
2 tablespoons honey
1½ tablespoons freshly squeezed lemon juice
1 tablespoon light corn syrup
1 tablespoon rice vinegar or white vinegar
2 teaspoons oil
2 teaspoons ketchup
1 clove garlic, minced
¼ teaspoon salt
Dash of white pepper
Peel of ¼ lemon

BATTER
4 tablespoons all-purpose flour
4 tablespoons water
2 tablespoons oil
¼ teaspoon baking soda

Oil for frying
½ lemon, thinly sliced, for garnish

1 Cut the chicken breast in half lengthwise and pound to flatten the thick part so the meat is of consistent thickness. Place the chicken in a shallow dish. In a small bowl, mix together the egg, 2 teaspoons of the cornstarch, 1 teaspoon of the salt, the pepper and the ginger. Pour the egg mixture over the chicken, turning the meat to coat all sides. Cover and refrigerate for 30 minutes, then remove the chicken, reserving the marinade.

2 Make the lemon sauce: Mix together the cornstarch and water in a small bowl. Combine the remaining sauce ingredients in a medium pan and bring to a boil. Add the cornstarch mixture to the sauce and cook, stirring continuously, until thickened, about 10 seconds. Remove from heat and remove the lemon peel.

3 Make the batter: In a shallow bowl, combine all batter ingredients until blended. Stir in the reserved marinade.

4 In a wok or deep skillet, heat 2 to 3 inches (5 to 7.5 cm) of the oil to 350°F (175°C). One at a time, dip the chicken pieces into the batter to coat all sides. Fry the chicken pieces for about 3 minutes, or until light brown, turning 2 or 3 times. Drain on a paper-towel-lined sheet pan.

5 Increase the oil temperature to 375°F (190°C). Re-fry all the chicken pieces at once until golden brown, turning once, about 2 minutes. Drain on paper-towel-lined sheet pan. Using a very sharp knife, cut each piece of chicken crosswise into ¾-in (2-cm) pieces. Transfer the chicken pieces to a serving platter.

6 Reheat the sauce over medium-high heat and pour over the chicken. Garnish with lemon slices and serve immediately with steaming-hot rice.

Kung Pao Chicken

This super-simple recipe puts the WOW in Kung Pao! You can make everyone's favorite stir-fry dish and have dinner on the table in minutes with this method. I used red bell pepper in this recipe, but it's fun to use a variety of bell pepper colors. Feel free to turn the heat level up a notch by doubling or tripling the amount of crushed red pepper flakes. You can easily substitute beef, pork or shrimp for the chicken, too.

Serves 4 to 6 as part of a multi-course meal
Preparation time: 10 minutes + marinating time
Cooking time: 7 minutes

SAUCE
2 tablespoons Chinese black vinegar
2 tablespoons chicken stock, homemade (page 62) or
    store-bought
1 teaspoon sugar
1½ tablespoons Chinese rice wine or sherry
1 tablespoon hoisin sauce, homemade (page 25) or
    store-bought
2 teaspoons oyster sauce
2 teaspoons soy sauce
1 teaspoon dark sesame oil
1 teaspoon all-purpose cornstarch
1 teaspoon water

12 oz (350 g) boneless, skinless chicken breast or thigh,
    cut into bite-sized pieces
¼ teaspoon salt
Dash of white pepper
1 teaspoon all-purpose cornstarch
2 tablespoons oil, divided
1 clove garlic, minced
½ teaspoon crushed red pepper
6 dried chilies or chiles de árbol
1 large red bell pepper, diced
2 tablespoons finely chopped green onion (scallion),
    white and green parts, plus more for garnish
½ cup (150 g) dry roasted peanuts, plus more for garnish

COOK'S NOTE
You may substitute balsamic vinegar for the
Chinese black vinegar if you wish.

1 Combine all of the sauce ingredients in a small bowl. Set aside.

2 Toss the chicken with the salt, pepper and cornstarch. Cover and refrigerate for 20 minutes.

3 Heat 1 tablespoon of the oil in a wok or skillet over medium-high heat. Add the chicken pieces and stir-fry until the chicken turns white, about 2 minutes. Remove the chicken from the pan and set aside.

4 Wash and thoroughly dry the wok or skillet, then heat the remaining 1 tablespoon oil over medium-high high heat. Add the garlic and stir-fry until fragrant, about 30 seconds. Add the crushed red pepper and dried red chilies and stir-fry until aromatic, about 1 minute.

5 Add the red bell pepper and stir-fry for 1 minute, then stir in the chicken and stir-fry for 2 minutes. Pour in the sauce and stir-fry for 1 minute, until the chicken is nicely coated. Add the peanuts and green onion and stir-fry for 30 seconds. Dish out and garnish with additional green onions and peanuts. Serve immediately with steaming-hot rice.

General Tso's Chicken

Legend has it that this popular sweet and slightly spicy chicken dish was named after a general and statesman from the Qing Dynasty named General Tso Tsung-tang. The reality is that this dish was invented by Chinese chefs who had immigrated to America; it was first introduced to New York City in the '70s. Whether or not you choose to believe the legend, everyone can agree that this dish has legendary flavor. In my mother's delicious recipe, the chicken is flash-fried, resulting in tender, juicy pieces which are then tossed in an addictive sauce made of soy sauce, rice vinegar, Chinese rice wine, garlic and ginger. This dish takes a bit more time than a simple stir-fry, but the results are totally worth it.

Serves 2 as a main dish with rice or 4 as part of a
   multi-course meal
Preparation time: 10 minutes
Cooking time: 6 to 7 minutes

2 teaspoons Chinese rice wine or sherry
2 teaspoons soy sauce
1 egg, lightly beaten
Dash of white pepper
2 tablespoons plus 2 teaspoons all-purpose cornstarch
8 oz (250 g) boneless, skinless chicken breast or thigh,
   cut into bite-sized pieces

SAUCE
1 tablespoon dark soy sauce
½ tablespoon rice vinegar or white vinegar
1 teaspoon Chinese rice wine or sherry
½ tablespoon sugar
1½ tablespoons chicken stock, homemade (page 62) or
   store-bought
2 teaspoons peeled and minced fresh ginger
1 clove garlic, minced
1 teaspoon all-purpose cornstarch

Oil for deep-frying, plus 1 tablespoon for stir-frying
1 clove garlic, minced
4 tablespoons finely chopped green onion (scallion),
   green and white parts, plus more for garnish
4 to 6 dried red chilies or chiles de árbol

COOK'S NOTE
You can substitute for dark soy sauce by
combining 1 part soy sauce mixed with 2 parts
brown sugar. Boil and let cool before using.

1 In a small bowl, mix together the rice wine or sherry, soy sauce, egg, white pepper and cornstarch. Add the chicken pieces and toss to coat.

2 Mix all sauce ingredients together in a small bowl. Set aside.

3 In a wok or deep skillet, heat 2 to 3 inches (5 to 7.5 cm) of the oil to 350°F (175°C). Fry the chicken pieces (4 to 5 at a time) for about 3 minutes, then transfer to a paper-towel-lined sheet pan.

4 Heat the remaining 1 tablespoon oil over medium-high heat. Add the garlic, green onion and dried chilies and stir-fry until fragrant, about 1 minute. Stir in the fried chicken and stir-fry for 1 minute more. Pour in the sauce and stir-fry until the chicken pieces are nicely coated, about 1 minute. Dish out and garnish with green onions. Serve immediately with steaming-hot rice.

Diced Chicken with Vegetables

My mother taught me that dicing all the ingredients in a stir-fry to approximately the same size ensures that everything is cooked evenly and quickly. Makes sense, right? It's also important to have everything cut, cleaned and ready to go before you fire up your wok. This is a great everyday weeknight dish because it's so easy to make, yet delicious and healthy. Feel free to substitute whatever veggies you like for those in the recipe. And if you have leftovers, use them to make a quick rice bowl for lunch the next day.

Serves 2 as a main dish with rice or
4 as part of a multi-course meal
Preparation time: 12 minutes +
marinating time
Cooking time: 10 minutes

10 oz (330 g) skinless, boneless chicken breast or thigh, cut into bite-sized cubes
½ teaspoon salt
Dash of white pepper
1 teaspoon plus 2 tablespoons all-purpose cornstarch, divided
½ cup (75 g) diced carrots
1 cup (100 g) diced celery
2 tablespoons oyster sauce
1¼ cups (295 ml) chicken stock, home-made (page 62) or store-bought, divided
½ teaspoon sugar
2 tablespoons oil, divided
4 tablespoons diced white onion
1 clove garlic, minced
1 teaspoon peeled and minced fresh ginger
½ cup (35 g) sliced white button mush-rooms
4 tablespoons finely chopped green onion (scallion), white and green parts

COOK'S NOTE
Use tofu in place of the chicken
and vegetable stock in place of
the chicken stock for a "Meatless
Monday" dish.

1 Toss the chicken with the salt, pepper and 1 teaspoon of the cornstarch. Cover and refrigerate for 20 minutes.

2 Blanch the carrots and celery in boiling water until tender, about 1 minute. Using a slotted spoon, transfer to an ice water bath to cool, then drain and set aside.

3 In a small bowl, combine the oyster sauce, the remaining 2 tablespoons cornstarch, 4 tablespoons of the chicken stock and the sugar. Set aside.

4 Heat 1 tablespoon of the oil in a wok or skillet over medium-high heat. Add the chicken pieces and stir-fry until the chicken turns white, about 2 minutes. Remove the chicken from the pan and set aside.

5 Wash and thoroughly dry the wok or skillet, then heat the remaining 1 tablespoon oil over medium-high heat. Add the onion, garlic and ginger and stir-fry until fragrant, about 1 minute. Add the celery, carrots and mushrooms and stir-fry for 1 minute.

6 Add the cooked chicken and the remaining 1 cup (125 ml) chicken stock. Cook until the stock comes to a boil. Stir in the cornstarch mixture and continue to cook, stirring continuously, until the sauce has thickened and all ingredients are nicely coated, about 2 minutes. Dish out and garnish with green onion. Serve immediately with steamed rice.

Chicken with Salted Black Beans, Tomatoes and Green Peppers

Salted black beans, also known as fermented black beans or dried black beans, are not the kind you find in Mexican cooking. They're actually soybeans which have been dried and fermented with salt and other spices, and sometimes chilies and wine. Because of their pungent flavor, they're used sparingly and paired with other strong flavors like garlic, onions and ginger. My mother and I threw a lot of dinner parties for my friends back in the day, and we always served a sparkling Shiraz with any dish with salted black beans. The bubbly wine offers a rich chocolate-and-cherry flavor that compliments black bean sauce rather overpowering it.

Serves 2 as a main dish with rice or 4 as part of a multi-course meal
Preparation time: 12 minutes + marinating time
Cooking time: 10 minutes

10 oz (330 g) skinless, boneless chicken breast or thigh, cut into bite-sized cubes
¼ teaspoon salt
Pinch white pepper
1 teaspoon plus 2 tablespoons all-purpose cornstarch, divided
2 tablespoons salted black beans
1 tablespoon sugar
½ cup (125 ml) chicken stock, homemade (page 62) or store-bought
2 teaspoons soy sauce
1 tablespoon oil
1 small white onion, diced
1 clove garlic, minced
1 teaspoon peeled and minced fresh ginger
3 small tomatoes, cut into wedges
1 small green bell pepper, diced

1 Toss the chicken with the salt, pepper and 1 teaspoon of the cornstarch. Cover and refrigerate for 30 minutes.

2 Place the beans in a small bowl and cover with warm water. Soak for 10 minutes, then remove and rinse with cold water to remove any excess salt and loosen the skins. Drain well.

3 In a small bowl, combine the remaining 2 tablespoons of cornstarch with the sugar, chicken stock and soy sauce. Set aside.

4 Heat the oil in a wok or skillet over medium-high heat. Add the chicken, onion, black beans, garlic and ginger and stir-fry for 2 minutes. Push the chicken to the sides of the wok or skillet and put the tomatoes and green pepper in the center. Stir-fry for 2 minutes more.

5 Add the cornstarch mixture and continue stir-frying the chicken, tomatoes and green pepper together until the sauce thickens and all ingredients are nicely coated. Dish out and serve immediately with steamed rice.

COOK'S NOTE
Salted black beans are available at Asian markets, but you can substitute an equal quantity of jarred black bean sauce, which is available at many grocery stores, if you wish.

Chicken with Shiitake Mushrooms and Snow Peas

City of Hope is a leading cancer research hospital based in Duarte, California. I'm very proud to be a Culinary Ambassador on behalf of their Super Foods initiative. This is an important cause for me, as my mother passed away from cancer. City of Hope has identified five foods with compounds that may prevent cancer as well as keep it from spreading and growing: mushrooms, pomegranates, blueberries, grapeseed extract and cinnamon. This dish is easy, delicious and loaded with shiitake mushrooms, a "superfood." Why not treat your family to this yummy dish tonight while potentially staving off cancer at the same time? That's not just smart, it's "super" smart!

Serves 2 as a main dish with rice or 4 as part of a multi-course meal
Preparation time: 12 minutes + marinating time
Cooking time: 10 minutes

10 oz (330 g) skinless, boneless chicken breast or thigh, cut into bite-sized cubes
¼ teaspoon salt
Dash of white pepper
3 teaspoons all-purpose cornstarch, divided
1½ cups (100 g) snow peas, tips and strings removed
2 teaspoons water
1 tablespoon oyster sauce
½ teaspoon sugar
2 tablespoons oil, divided
1 clove garlic, minced
1 teaspoon peeled and minced fresh ginger
1½ cups (100 g) fresh shiitake mushrooms, stemmed and thinly sliced
½ cup (125 ml) chicken stock, homemade (page 62) or store-bought
½ green onion (scallion), trimmed and cut into thin strips, for garnish

1 Toss the chicken with the salt, pepper and 1 teaspoon cornstarch. Cover and refrigerate for 30 minutes.

2 Blanch the snow peas in boiling water until tender, about 1 minute. Using a slotted spoon, transfer to an ice water bath to cool, then drain and set aside.

3 In a small bowl, combine the remaining 2 teaspoons cornstarch with the 2 teaspoons water, oyster sauce and sugar.

4 Heat 1 tablespoon of the oil in a wok or skillet over medium-high heat. Add the chicken pieces and stir-fry until the chicken turns white, about 2 minutes. Remove the chicken from the pan and set aside.

5 Wash and thoroughly dry the wok or skillet, then heat the remaining 1 tablespoon oil over medium-high heat. Add the garlic and ginger and stir-fry until fragrant, about 30 seconds. Add the mushrooms and stir-fry for 1 minute. Add the chicken stock and chicken pieces. Cook until the stock comes to a boil, then add the cornstarch mixture and continue to stir-fry until the sauce has thickened and all the ingredients are nicely coated.

6 Add the reserved snow peas and stir-fry for 30 seconds more. Dish out and garnish with green onion. Serve immediately with steamed rice.

Stir-fried Chicken with Bok Choy

Did you know that bok choy is super-duper nutrient-dense? It's loaded with vitamin A, anti-oxidants and Omega-3s. I think my mother was ahead of her time. She cooked bok choy for us at least once a week. She knew she had to build up our immune systems for the harsh Minnesota winters! This delicious and healthful dish is easy to make. Serve it with steaming-hot brown rice for an even more nutritious meal.

Serves 2 as a main dish with rice or 4 as part of a multi-course meal
Preparation time: 12 minutes + marinating time
Cooking time: 10 minutes

10 oz (330 g) skinless, boneless chicken breast or thigh, cut into bite-sized cubes
½ teaspoon salt, divided
Dash of white pepper
4 teaspoons all-purpose cornstarch, divided
4 oz (100 g) snow peas, tips and strings removed
2 tablespoons oyster sauce
½ teaspoon sugar
3 tablespoons oil, divided
1 teaspoon peeled and minced fresh ginger
1 garlic clove, minced
4 stalks bok choy, trimmed and cut diagonally into ½-in (1.25-cm) slices
1 small red bell pepper, thinly sliced
½ cup (125 ml) chicken stock, homemade (page 62) or store-bought

COOK'S NOTE
You may use baby bok choy if you prefer, but cut it into 1-inch (2.5-cm) pieces instead of thin slices.

1 Toss the chicken with ¼ teaspoon of the salt, the pepper and 1 teaspoon of the cornstarch. Cover and refrigerate for 30 minutes.

2 Blanch the snow peas in boiling water until tender, about 1 minute. Use a slotted spoon to transfer the snow peas to an ice water bath to cool, then drain and set aside.

3 In a small bowl, combine the oyster sauce, sugar, the remaining 3 teaspoons cornstarch and 1 tablespoon water. Set aside.

4 Heat 1½ tablespoons of the oil in a wok or skillet over medium-high heat. Add the chicken pieces and stir-fry until the chicken turns white, about 2 minutes. Remove the chicken from the pan and set aside.

5 Wash and thoroughly dry the wok or skillet, then heat the remaining 1½ tablespoons oil over medium-high heat. Add the ginger and garlic and stir-fry until fragrant, about 30 seconds. Add the bok choy and red pepper and stir-fry for 1 minute. Add the remaining ¼ teaspoon salt, the chicken stock and the chicken. Cook until the stock comes to a boil. Add the cornstarch mixture and stir until the sauce thickens and all the ingredients are nicely coated. Add the snow peas and stir-fry for 30 seconds. Dish out and serve immediately with steamed rice.

Beef, Pork and Lamb

My mother always made a special beef dish when many of my siblings came home from college. It was her way of saying "I love you" or "Good job on your straight As, Jeanie." (That was for my sister—when I came home with straight B's, she made squab.) Beef was a luxury in our home, and my mother had rarely eaten it when she was growing up in China because it was scarce. The beef dishes she made always melted in our mouths; she chose fine cuts and always cut across the grain. Once she opened her first restaurant, my mother went wild creating beef dishes, as there are so many delicious ways to prepare beef in Chinese cuisine. I've included some of my mother's legendary beef recipes, like the tender and succulent Stir-Fried Beef with Asparagus and Wild Mushrooms (page 94) and the spicy Sichuan Beef (page 90).

Pork, on the other hand, we ate all the time: it's a healthy lean protein and its rich taste goes really well with Chinese flavors. In fact, "pork" is literally synonymous with "meat" in Chinese, and it's ubiquitous in China, much more so than beef. It's always eaten on Chinese New Year because its richness symbolizes prosperity. Pork can be prepared in so many ways—steamed, braised, fried, roasted and baked—and it's incredibly versatile, from the crispy and tender Sweet-and-Sour Pork (page 86) to the classic Chinese comfort food, Mapo Tofu (page 97).

Finally, I just had to include one of my mom's favorite lamb dishes in this section. Her Mongolian Lamb (page 96) is warming and savory, and will satisfy any warrior-sized appetite.

Sweet-and-Sour Pork

When I was in second grade, I opened my lunch box to find a *char siu bao* (barbecued pork bun) and some soy-sauce chicken wings. One mean girl named Penny laughed at my weird lunch, and all the other bologna-eating children joined in. A couple of weeks later, my mother cooked my favorite dish, Sweet-and-Sour Pork, for my seventh birthday party. The children gasped in amazement as she created a dish they thought could only be made at a restaurant. And boy, it was good—filled with tender, crispy pork pieces in a delicious sweet-and-sour glaze. The next day, I opened my lunch box and revealed four *shu mai* dumplings. Instead of laughing, Penny said, "Could I try one of those things?"

Serves 4 to 6 as part of a multi-course meal
Preparation time: 30 minutes + marinating time
Cooking time: 25 minutes

1 large egg, slightly beaten
1 tablespoon all-purpose cornstarch
1 tablespoon oil
1 teaspoon salt
1 teaspoon soy sauce
¼ teaspoon white pepper
12 oz (350 g) boneless pork loin, cut into 1-in (2.5-cm)
    cubes
Oil for frying

SWEET-AND-SOUR SAUCE
4 tablespoons cold water
3 tablespoons all-purpose cornstarch
1 cup sugar
¾ cup (185 ml) chicken stock, homemade
    (page 62) or store-bought
¾ cup (185 ml) white vinegar
1 tablespoon oil
2 teaspoons dark soy sauce
1 teaspoon salt
1 clove garlic, minced
1 small tomato, cut into wedges
1 small green bell pepper, cut into 1-in
    (2.5-cm) chunks
One 8¼-oz (250 g) can pineapple chunks, drained

BATTER
4 tablespoons all-purpose flour
4 tablespoons water
1 tablespoons all-purpose cornstarch
2 teaspoons oil
¼ teaspoon baking soda

1 In a medium bowl, combine the egg, 1 tablespoon cornstarch, 1 tablespoon oil, 1 teaspoon salt, 1 teaspoon soy sauce and white pepper. Add the pork pieces and toss to coat. Cover and refrigerate for 20 minutes. Transfer the pork to a bowl or plate, reserving the marinade.

2 Make the sweet-and-sour sauce: Combine the water and cornstarch in a small bowl. Bring the sugar, chicken stock, vinegar, oil, dark soy sauce, salt and garlic to a boil in a saucepan. Stir in the cornstarch mixture and cook, stirring continuously, for about 20 seconds or until thickened. Stir in the tomatoes, bell pepper and pineapple. Remove the sauce from heat.

3 Make the batter: In a large bowl, combine all batter ingredients and mix until blended. Stir in the reserved marinade. Add the pork pieces to the batter and stir until well coated.

4 Heat 2 to 3 inches (5 to 7.5 cm) of the oil in a wok or deep skillet to 350°F (175°C). Fry about 15 pieces at a time, turning frequently, until light brown, about 4 minutes. Drain on a paper-towel-lined sheet pan. Increase oil temperature to 375°F (190°C). Fry the pork pieces all at one time for 1 minute more, or until golden brown. Drain on a paper-towel-lined sheet pan. Transfer the pork pieces to a platter.

5 Reheat the sauce over medium-high heat and pour over the pork. Serve immediately with steaming-hot rice.

Hong Kong Steak

When my mother moved to Hong Kong to be married to my father through the services of a matchmaker, she was thrust into a new life in a cosmopolitan city with someone she had literally just met, not to mention a mother-in-law who tagged along for the ride. Living in their new apartment, my mother threw herself into cooking, coming up with dishes she hoped her new husband and mother-in-law would approve of. She told me she'd serve Hong Kong Steak to the unexpected dinner guests my father would frequently bring home; it was quick to make and unfailingly delicious. Whether you're cooking for your family or unexpected guests, this succulent and tender dish is sure to get rave reviews.

Serves 6 as part of a multi-course meal
Preparation time: 15 minutes +
* marinating time*
Cooking time: 15 to 25 minutes,
* depending on steak thickness*

1½ lbs (750 g) beef tenderloin
2 tablespoons oil
1 teaspoon soy sauce
1 teaspoon salt
3 cloves garlic, minced
1 tablespoon peeled and minced fresh ginger
1 teaspoon sugar
1 teaspoon ground red pepper (cayenne)
4 tablespoons hoisin sauce, homemade
  (page 25) or store-bought

1 Place the beef in a large resealable plastic food storage bag. Combine all remaining ingredients in a small bowl and whisk to blend. Pour over the beef, seal the bag, and place it in the refrigerator for at least 30 minutes or as long as overnight.

2 Preheat a grill to high heat and brush with oil. Remove the beef from the marinade and grill to desired doneness, about 4 to 5 minutes per side for medium-rare, depending on thickness. Let rest for 10 minutes.

3 Slice beef thinly and serve immediately.

Hoisin Lacquered Ribs

When my husband and I started dating, he enjoyed meeting my mom for the first time. But when she made her Hoisin Lacquered Ribs for him, he fell in love with her (I had secretly coaxed her into making his favorite food). Because this potential son-in-law showed so much enthusiasm for her food, she fell in love with him. That did it for me, too: one way to a Chinese woman's heart is to become infatuated with her mother's cooking. Anyway, I guarantee you'll fall in love with these fall-off-the-bone ribs prepared with a simple Chinese marinade of hoisin sauce, white wine, garlic, ketchup, sugar and salt. They are glistening, tender and completely addictive.

Serves 4 as part of a multi-course meal
Preparation time: 10 minutes +
*   marinating time*
Cooking time: 60 minutes

2½ to 3 lbs (1.25 to 1.5 kg) baby back ribs
½ cup (125 ml) ketchup
2 tablespoons sugar
2 tablespoons hoisin sauce, homemade
    (page 25) or store-bought
1 tablespoon dry white wine
2 teaspoons salt
2 cloves garlic, minced

1 Trim fat and remove membrane from ribs, then place them in a shallow dish. Mix remaining ingredients together and pour over ribs, turning to coat. Cover and refrigerate at least 2 hours, but no longer than 24 hours.

2 Heat oven to 400°F (200°C). Place ribs in a single layer on a rack in a roasting pan and brush with the marinade sauce. Bake, uncovered, for 30 minutes. Turn ribs and brush with more sauce, then continue baking until done, about 30 minutes longer. (Reduce oven temperature to 375°F (190°C) for the last 30 minutes if ribs are thin.) Cut ribs apart and serve with hot mustard if desired.

Sichuan Beef

The province of Sichuan is known for its hot chili peppers and hot chili oil, both of which flavor its world-renowned spicy dishes. Filled with succulent strips of beef, this dish is distinctly flavored with chili oil, chili paste and Sichuan peppercorns, but it's not too hot and spicy—at least according to my 12 year-old nephew Jack, who was a taste-tester during a recent family reunion in Minneapolis (a lot of families eat "Aunt Nancy's" potato salad at family reunions, but we eat Sichuan Beef). Jack said, "This dish is complex, with layers of heat, but it's not overpowering"—and yes, that day a food critic was born.

Serves 2 as a main dish with rice, or 4 as part of a multi-course meal
Preparation time: 10 minutes + marinating time
Cooking time: 5 minutes

12 oz (350 g) top sirloin, beef tenderloin, or flank steak, cut across the grain into thin strips
1 teaspoon plus 1 tablespoon oil, divided
1 teaspoon all-purpose cornstarch
½ teaspoon salt
Dash of white pepper
2 teaspoons chili paste
2 teaspoons soy sauce
1 tablespoon Chinese rice wine or sherry
1 tablespoon water
½ teaspoon sugar
½ teaspoon hot chili oil, homemade (page 25) or store-bought
2 teaspoons peeled and minced fresh ginger
2 cloves garlic, minced
3 green onions (scallions), white part only, cut into thin shreds
1 carrot, cut into matchsticks
½ teaspoon roasted Sichuan peppercorns (optional)
Thinly sliced green onions, for garnish

COOK'S NOTE
To roast Sichuan peppercorns, place them in a frying pan over medium-low heat. Roast, shaking the pan occasionally, until they begin to darken and become fragrant. Remove from pan and cool. Store leftover roasted peppercorns in a covered jar.

1 Toss the beef with 1 teaspoon of the oil, the all-purpose cornstarch, salt, and white pepper in a small bowl. Cover and refrigerate for 10 minutes.

2 In a small bowl, mix together the chili paste, soy sauce, rice wine or sherry, water, sugar and chili oil. Set aside.

3 Heat the remaining 1 tablespoon oil in a wok or skillet over medium-high heat. Add the ginger, garlic and green onions and stir-fry until fragrant, about 1 minute. Add the beef and stir-fry until the meat browns, about 2 minutes. Stir in the carrots and stir-fry for another minute, then add the chili paste mixture and stir-fry until combined, about 1 minute. Add the Sichuan peppercorns, if using, and toss to combine. Dish out and garnish with green onion. Serve immediately with jasmine rice.

Stir-Fried Beef with Tomato

"Melt-in-your-mouth yumminess nom nom nom" is how my niece Katie (who shares not only my name, but my taste in nail polish colors) described this dish. She had just moved to Los Angeles and was missing some of the comfort food her Pah Pah (Chinese for "grandmother") used to make. Most of the dishes we regard as comfort food in our family are the simplest, like this Stir-Fried Beef with Tomato. The tender and succulent beef is quickly stir-fried with juicy, ripe tomatoes, onions and garlic with a bit of hoisin sauce. Pah Pah always taught us that by using the freshest ingredients and good cuts of meat, you can never go wrong.

Serves 2 as a main dish with rice or 4 as part of a multi-course meal
Preparation time: 8 minutes + marinating time
Cooking time: 5 minutes

10 oz (330 g) beef tenderloin, top sirloin or flank steak, sliced diagonally across the grain in ¼-in (6-mm) slices
3 teaspoons all-purpose cornstarch, divided
4 teaspoons oil, divided
¼ teaspoon salt
Dash of white pepper
1 tablespoon water
1 clove garlic, minced
1 small white onion, cut into cubes
2 tablespoons hoisin sauce, homemade (page 25) or store-bought
2 medium tomatoes, cut into wedges

COOK'S NOTE
To make the beef easier to slice thinly, place it in the freezer for 30 minutes before preparing this recipe.

1 Toss the beef with 1 teaspoon of the cornstarch, 1 teaspoon of the oil, and the salt and pepper. Cover and refrigerate for 20 minutes.

2 In a small bowl, combine the remaining 3 teaspoons cornstarch and 1 tablespoon water. Set aside.

3 Heat the remaining 3 teaspoons of the oil in a wok or skillet over medium-high heat. Add the beef, garlic, and onion and stir-fry for 1 to 2 minutes. Stir in the hoisin sauce and the cornstarch mixture. When the mixture begins to thicken (about 1 minute), add the tomatoes and stir-fry for another minute. Dish out and serve immediately with steaming-hot rice.

Tangerine Beef

When I was growing up, I remember my mother scattering tangerine peels on our kitchen windowsill so they'd dry out in the sun. You can dry tangerine peels yourself—just take off any stickers and remove the pith from the peels, then set them out on a sheet pan for several days until they're crisp and dry. Of course, it may be easier and more convenient to buy dried tangerine peel from your nearest Asian market. I love the complex layered flavors that the rice wine, Sichuan peppercorns and dried chilies contribute to this dish, with the sweet-tart flavors of the tangerine juice and peel mingling together with tender, juicy slices of beef.

Serves 4 to 6 as part of a multi-course meal
Preparation time: 10 minutes + soaking marinating time
Cooking time: 6 minutes

Three 2 x 1.5-in (5 x 3.75-cm) pieces dried tangerine peel, cut into ½-in (1.25-cm) matchsticks
12 oz (350 g) beef tenderloin, top sirloin or flank steak, thinly sliced across the grain
1 teaspoon plus 2 tablespoons oil, divided
3 teaspoons all-purpose cornstarch, divided
½ teaspoon salt
Dash of white pepper
2 teaspoons hoisin sauce, homemade (page 25) or store-bought
4 tablespoons freshly squeezed tangerine juice or orange juice
1 tablespoon soy sauce
1 tablespoon Chinese rice wine or sherry
1 teaspoon sugar
2 teaspoons chili garlic sauce
2 tablespoons oil, divided
6 dried chilies or chiles de árbol
1 clove garlic, minced
1 teaspoon peeled and minced fresh ginger
1 small onion, cut into 1-in (2.5-cm) cubes
½ teaspoon roasted Sichuan peppercorns (optional)
½ cup (50 g) finely chopped green onion (scallion), white and green parts
Orange slices for garnish

1 Soak dried tangerine peel in warm water to cover until softened, about 15 minutes. Drain and slice thinly.

2 Toss the beef with 1 teaspoon of the oil, 1 teaspoon of the cornstarch, the salt and the white pepper. Cover and refrigerate for 10 minutes.

3 In a small bowl, whisk together the hoisin sauce, tangerine or orange juice, soy sauce, rice wine or sherry, sugar, chili garlic sauce and the remaining 2 teaspoons cornstarch. Set aside.

4 Heat 1 tablespoon of the oil in a wok or skillet over medium-high heat. Add the dried chilies and stir-fry for 1 minute. Remove with a slotted spoon and set aside.

5 Heat the remaining oil in the same pan over medium-high heat. Add the garlic, ginger and onion and stir-fry until fragrant, about 1 minute. Stir in the beef and stir-fry until the meat browns, about 2 minutes. Pour in the hoisin sauce mixture and stir-fry until combined, about 1 minute. Add the tangerine peel and the Sichuan peppercorns, if using, and stir-fry for 1 minute more. Dish out and garnish with orange slices. Serve immediately with jasmine rice.

COOK'S NOTE
To roast Sichuan peppercorns, place them in a frying pan over medium-low heat. Roast, shaking the pan occasionally, until they begin to darken and become fragrant. Remove from the pan and cool. Store leftover roast peppercorns in a covered jar.

Stir-Fried Beef with Broccoli

My friends who are parents often say the only time their kids will eat broccoli is when it's in Beef with Broccoli from Chinese takeout, and they've begged me for an easy recipe they can make at home. You asked for it, guys—you got it! This recipe is so simple anyone can make it (you probably already have most of the ingredients in your pantry) and it's so quick that you can get dinner on the table in a flash. The secret is blanching the broccoli in advance so it's tender-crisp when it hits the pan, but not overcooking it.

Serves 2 as a main dish with rice or 4 as part of a multi-course meal
Preparation time: 12 minutes + marinating time
Cooking time: 5 minutes

8 oz (250 g) beef tenderloin, top sirloin or flank steak, sliced diagonally across the grain in ¼-in (6-mm) slices
1 teaspoon plus 1 tablespoon oil, divided
½ teaspoon plus 1 tablespoon all-purpose cornstarch, divided
¾ teaspoon salt, divided
½ teaspoon sugar
½ teaspoon soy sauce
Dash of white pepper
8 oz (250 g) broccoli florets
4 tablespoons chicken stock, homemade (page 62) or store-bought, divided
1 tablespoons oyster sauce
1 teaspoon peeled and minced fresh ginger
1 clove garlic, minced

COOK'S NOTE
You can save time and minimize waste by purchasing pre-cut broccoli florets from the salad bar at your local grocery store.

1 Toss the beef with 1 teaspoon of the oil, ½ teaspoon of the cornstarch, ½ teaspoon of the salt, and the sugar, soy sauce and white pepper. Cover and refrigerate for 20 minutes.

2 Blanch the broccoli in boiling water until tender, about 1 minute. Using a slotted spoon, transfer to an ice water bath to cool, then drain and set aside.

3 In a small bowl, mix 2 tablespoons of the chicken stock, the oyster sauce and the remaining 1 tablespoon cornstarch. Set aside.

4 Heat the remaining 1 tablespoon of oil in a wok or skillet over medium-high heat. Add the beef, ginger and garlic and stir-fry until fragrant, about 1 minute. Stir in the blanched broccoli and the remaining ¼ teaspoon salt and stir-fry for 1 minute.

5 Pour in the remaining 2 tablespoons of chicken stock. When it comes to a boil, add the cornstarch mixture and cook until the sauce thickens and all the ingredients are nicely coated, about 30 seconds. Dish out and serve immediately with steaming-hot rice.

Stir-fried Beef with Asparagus and Wild Mushrooms

Whenever I returned home from college, I'd make my mom drive straight to one of her elegant buffet restaurants so I could dive right into a plate of her Stir-Fried Beef with Asparagus and Wild Mushrooms. Dorm food was a far cry from my mother's cooking, and this was one of her dishes I missed the most. As soon as I caught a whiff of this succulent beef dish loaded with asparagus and wild mushrooms stir-fried in a rich, yet light gravy, I knew I was finally home.

*Serves 2 as a main dish with rice or
4 as part of a multi-course meal*
*Preparation time: 10 minutes +
marinating time*
Cooking time: 5 minutes

8 oz (250 g) beef tenderloin, sirloin steak
  or flank steak, sliced diagonally across
  the grain in ¼-in (6-mm) slices
1 teaspoon plus 1 tablespoon oil, divided
½ teaspoon plus 1 tablespoon all-purpose
  cornstarch, divided
1 teaspoon salt, divided
½ teaspoon sugar
½ teaspoon soy sauce
Dash of white pepper
4 tablespoons chicken stock, homemade
  (page 62) or store-bought, divided
1 tablespoon oyster sauce
1 teaspoon peeled and minced fresh
  ginger
1 clove garlic, minced
4 oz (100 g) fresh shiitake or oyster
  mushrooms, stemmed and thinly sliced
6 oz (175 g) asparagus, ends trimmed and
  cut into 2-in (5-cm) pieces
1 tablespoon white wine
1 green onion (scallion), cut into 1-in
  (2.5-cm) pieces, for garnish

1 Toss the beef with 1 teaspoon of the oil, ½ teaspoon of the cornstarch, ½ teaspoon of the salt, and the sugar, soy sauce and white pepper. Cover and refrigerate for 20 minutes.

2 In a small bowl, combine 2 tablespoons of the chicken stock, the remaining 1 tablespoon cornstarch and the oyster sauce. Set aside.

3 Heat the remaining 1 tablespoon oil in a wok or skillet. Add the beef, ginger and garlic and stir-fry for 1 to 2 minutes. Stir in the mushrooms and asparagus and the remaining ½ teaspoon salt and stir-fry for 1 minute. Pour in the white wine and stir-fry for 30 seconds.

4 Add the remaining 2 tablespoons chicken stock. When the liquid comes to a boil, add the cornstarch mixture and cook until the sauce thickens and all the ingredients are nicely coated, about 15 seconds. Dish out and garnish with green onions. Serve immediately with steaming-hot rice.

Pepper Steak

One Valentine's day back in my single days, my mom helped me throw a Sgt. Pepper's Lonely Hearts Club dinner for all of my single LA friends. We made Pepper Steak in honor of Sgt. Pepper. Ironically, anytime anyone eats Pepper Steak, they are very much *not* alone—it's beloved by millions. Bursting with color from the bell peppers, this yummy dish marries simple ingredients like ginger, garlic and onions with tender steak. The tender and flavorful result is impossible not to love.

Serves 2 as a main dish with rice or 4 as part of a multi-course meal
Preparation time: 10 minutes + marinating time
Cooking time: 5 minutes

8 oz (250 g) beef tenderloin, top sirloin or flank steak, sliced diagonally across the grain in ¼-in (6-mm) slices
1 teaspoon plus 1 tablespoon oil, divided
½ teaspoon plus 1 tablespoon all-purpose cornstarch, divided
½ teaspoon salt
½ teaspoon soy sauce
Dash of white pepper
4 tablespoons chicken stock, homemade (page 62) or store-bought, divided
1 tablespoon dark soy sauce
½ teaspoon sugar
1 clove garlic, minced
1 teaspoon peeled and minced fresh ginger
½ cup (45 g) red bell pepper, cut into 1-in (2.5-cm) chunks
½ cup (45 g) green bell pepper, cut into 1-in (2.5-cm) chunks
1 small onion, diced

1 Toss the beef with 1 teaspoon of the oil, ½ teaspoon of the cornstarch, and the salt, soy sauce and white pepper. Cover and refrigerate for 20 minutes.

2 In a small bowl, mix 2 tablespoons of the chicken stock, the remaining 1 tablespoon of the cornstarch, the dark soy sauce and the sugar together until blended. Set aside.

3 Heat the remaining 1 tablespoon of oil in a wok or skillet over medium-high heat. Add the beef, garlic and ginger and stir-fry for 1 to 2 minutes. Add the bell peppers and onion and stir-fry for 1 minute.

4 Add the remaining 2 tablespoons of chicken stock and heat to boiling. Pour in the cornstarch mixture and continue to stir-fry until the sauce thickens and all the ingredients are nicely coated. Serve immediately with steaming hot jasmine rice.

Mongolian Lamb

I've been told that Mongolian Lamb is a Chinese-American dish invented by Chinese restaurateurs. While it isn't an authentic dish from China or Mongolia, it's made with classic Chinese seasonings, and because it's a popular restaurant dish, it's been woven into the fabric of Chinese-American cuisine. It's usually made with beef, but my nephew Logan gave me the idea to switch it up with lamb for this recipe. Tender pieces of meat are stir-fried in a savory garlic-ginger brown sauce, finishing with some nice heat from the crushed red pepper. You can substitute beef or pork for the lamb if you wish.

Serves 2 as a main dish with rice or 4 as part of a multi-course meal
Preparation time: 8 minutes + marinating time
Cooking time: 4 minutes

8 oz (250 g) boneless leg of lamb, cut into thin strips
1 teaspoon all-purpose cornstarch
5 teaspoons oil, divided
1 teaspoon sugar
½ teaspoon salt
¼ teaspoon white pepper
½ teaspoon crushed red pepper
½ tablespoon brown bean paste
1 clove garlic, minced
1 teaspoon peeled and minced fresh ginger
1 teaspoon dark soy sauce
1 green onion (scallion), cut diagonally into 1-in (2.5-cm) pieces

1 Toss the lamb with the cornstarch, 1 teaspoon of the oil, the sugar, salt and white pepper. Cover and refrigerate for 30 minutes.

2 Heat the remaining 4 teaspoons of oil in a wok or skillet over medium-high heat. Add the crushed red pepper, bean paste, garlic and ginger and stir-fry for 30 seconds. Stir in the lamb and stir-fry for 2 minutes. Add the soy sauce and green onions and stir-fry for another 30 seconds. Dish out and serve immediately with steaming-hot rice.

COOK'S NOTE
Hoisin sauce can be used in place of the brown bean paste; if you do so, reduce the sugar by half.

Mapo Tofu

My mother's father told her the folktale associated with this ubiquitous Sichuan dish, whose name means "pockmarked grandmother's bean curd." According to the story, an old Sichuan woman with a pockmarked face opened a restaurant without a name. People would travel great distances for her delicious tofu dish, but because her restaurant was nameless, they named the dish after her features. Whatever you call it, this dish is filled with juicy ground pork stir-fried with tofu in a spicy and savory sauce, and it's amazing served over rice. It's one of my go-to comfort foods from my childhood, and I hope it makes a name for itself in your family, too.

Serves 4 as part of a multi-course meal
Preparation time: 10 minutes + soaking time
Cooking time: 7 minutes

1 tablespoon fermented black beans
One 14-oz (400-g) block firm tofu, drained, patted dry and cut into cubes
¼ teaspoon salt
⅛ teaspoon white pepper
1 teaspoon all-purpose cornstarch
2 tablespoons oil
8 oz (250 g) ground pork
1 teaspoon soy sauce
2 tablespoons brown bean paste
1 tablespoon chili oil, homemade (page 25) or store-bought
2 cloves garlic, minced
1 tablespoon hoisin sauce, homemade (page 25) or store-bought
1 teaspoon sugar
1 teaspoon ground red pepper (cayenne)
2 green onions (scallions), white and green parts, finely chopped, for garnish

1 Place the black beans in a small bowl and cover with warm water. Stir the beans for about 2 minutes to remove the excess salt, then remove from the water, rinse and drain well. Set aside.

2 In a separate bowl, gently toss the tofu with the salt, pepper and cornstarch.

3 Heat the oil in a wok or skillet over medium-high heat. Add the tofu and stir-fry until light brown, about 3 minutes. Remove from pan and set aside. Add the ground pork, rinsed black beans and soy sauce and continue to stir-fry until the pork turns white, about 2 minutes. Stir in the brown bean paste, chili oil, garlic, hoisin sauce, sugar and cayenne. Stir-fry for 30 seconds, then add the tofu to the pork mixture. Cook for 1 minute. Dish out and garnish with green onions. Serve immediately with steaming-hot rice.

COOK'S NOTE
Hoisin sauce may be substituted for the brown bean paste. If you do so, reduce sugar the by half.

Stir-Fried Beef with Snow Peas and Red Bell Pepper

When my sister Jeanie was in medical school, she barely got any sleep and was working crazy hours. She had lost weight and looked tired, and my mother was determined to get her back on track with protein- and iron-rich stir-fries. One of her favorites was this Stir-Fried Beef with Snow Peas and Red Bell Pepper. It's healthy and delicious, filled with tender-crisp snow peas, crunchy red bell pepper and succulent beef. My mother would invite my sister over for dinner and insist on picking her up and driving her home. She'd keep offering Jeanie seconds and thirds (which no dutiful daughter would dream of turning down) until she felt satisfied that Jeanie had eaten enough, at which point she'd finally drive her home.

Serves 2 as a main dish with rice or 4 as part of a multi-course meal
Preparation time: 12 minutes + marinating time
Cooking time: 5 minutes

8 oz (250 g) beef tenderloin or boneless sirloin steak, sliced diagonally across the grain in ¼-in (6-mm) slices
1 teaspoon plus 1 tablespoon oil, divided
½ teaspoon plus 1 tablespoon all-purpose cornstarch, divided
1 teaspoon salt, divided
1 teaspoon sugar, divided
½ teaspoon soy sauce
Dash of white pepper
2 oz (50 g) snow peas, tips and strings removed
4 tablespoons chicken stock, homemade (page 62) or store-bought, divided
1 tablespoon oyster sauce
1 teaspoon peeled and minced fresh ginger
1 clove garlic, minced
½ cup (40 g) sliced mushrooms
2 stalks bok choy, trimmed and cut diagonally into ½-in (1.25-cm) slices
½ cup (85 g) thinly sliced red bell pepper
2 oz (50 g) sliced canned water chestnuts
2 oz (50 g) sliced canned bamboo shoots
1 teaspoon dry white wine

1 Toss the beef with 1 teaspoon of the oil, ½ teaspoon of the cornstarch, ½ teaspoon of the salt, ½ teaspoon of the sugar, the soy sauce and the white pepper. Cover and refrigerate for 20 minutes.

2 Blanch the snow peas in boiling water until tender, about 1 minute. Using a slotted spoon, transfer the snow peas to an ice water bath to cool, then drain and set aside.

3 In a small bowl, combine 2 tablespoons of the chicken stock, the remaining 1 tablespoon cornstarch, oyster sauce and the remaining ½ teaspoon sugar. Set aside.

4 Heat the remaining 1 tablespoon of oil in a wok or skillet over medium-high heat. Add the beef, ginger and garlic and stir-fry for 2 minutes. Stir in the mushrooms, bok choy, red bell pepper, water chestnuts, bamboo shoots and the remaining ½ teaspoon salt and stir-fry for 1 to 2 minutes more.

5 Add the white wine and stir-fry for 30 seconds, then pour in the remaining 2 tablespoons chicken stock. When the stock comes to a boil, pour in the cornstarch mixture and cook until the sauce thickens and all the ingredients are nicely coated, about 15 seconds. Dish out and serve immediately with steaming-hot rice.

COOK'S NOTE
To make the beef easier to slice thinly, place it in the freezer for 30 minutes before preparing the recipe.

Stir-Fried Pork with Zucchini

File this one under "Easy-peasy." My mother always had zucchini on hand for stir-fries. Because of its delicate flavor, it pairs well with almost any protein. It cooks quickly, so there's no blanching required, making it a snap for a busy weeknight. I like to combine yellow and green zucchini for a colorful dish.

Serves 2 as a main dish with rice or 4 as part of a
*   multi-course meal*
Preparation time: 10 minutes + marinating and
*   soaking time*
Cooking time: 5 minutes

8 oz (250 g) pork loin or pork tenderloin, cut into ½-in (1.25-cm) pieces
¼ teaspoon salt
Dash of white pepper
½ teaspoon plus 2 teaspoons all-purpose cornstarch, divided
4 dried black mushrooms
2 teaspoons water
1 tablespoon oyster sauce
¼ teaspoon sugar
1 tablespoon oil
1 clove garlic, minced
2 to 3 small zucchini, sliced diagonally into ¼-in (6-mm) slices
4 tablespoons chicken stock, homemade (page 62) or store-bought

1 Toss the pork with the salt, pepper and ½ teaspoon of the cornstarch. Cover and refrigerate for 20 minutes.

2 Soak the black mushrooms in hot water for 20 minutes, or until soft. Cut off the stems and discard. Cut the mushroom caps into ½-inch (1.25-cm) pieces.

3 In a small bowl, combine the remaining 2 teaspoons of the cornstarch with the water, oyster sauce and sugar. Set aside.

4 Heat the oil in a wok or skillet over medium-high heat. Add the pork and garlic and stir-fry for 2 minutes. Stir in the zucchini and black mushrooms and stir-fry for 2 minutes.

5 Pour in the chicken stock and cook until the stock comes to a boil. Add the cornstarch mixture and cook for about 30 seconds more, until the sauce thickens and all the ingredients are nicely coated. Dish out and serve immediately with steaming-hot rice.

Pork Tenderloin with Wild Mushrooms

If you love mushrooms, this is for you. It's different than the usual stir-fry, as the pork medallions are dusted with cornstarch and pan-fried a bit before the other ingredients are added. I love the slightly crisp texture of the pork mixed with the sumptuous and tender shiitake and oyster mushrooms in the velvety gravy. When I made this, I heard my six year-old daughter Becca say, "Umami," which made me so proud, but my husband later told me she actually said, "Oooh, mommy!"

Serves 2 as a main dish with rice or 4 as part of a multi-course meal
Preparation time: 15 minutes + marinating time
Cooking time: 10 minutes

10 oz (330 g) pork tenderloin, cut into ½-in (1.25-cm) pieces
1 teaspoon salt, divided
¼ teaspoon white pepper
2 tablespoons all-purpose cornstarch
3 tablespoons oil, divided
1 clove garlic, minced
3 to 4 celery stalks, cut into ¼-in (6-mm) diagonal slices
4 tablespoons chicken stock, homemade (page 62) or store-bought
2 oz (50 g) shiitake mushrooms
2 oz (50 g) oyster mushrooms
2 tablespoons oyster sauce
3 green onions (scallions), chopped (white and green parts)

1 Sprinkle ½ teaspoon of the salt and the pepper over the pork pieces. Place them on a plate or wax paper. Dip each piece of tenderloin in cornstarch to coat.

2 Heat 2 tablespoons of the oil in a wok or skillet over medium-high heat. Place the pork slices in the pan in a single layer, not overlapping. (If the pan is not large enough, cook the pork in batches.) Fry until golden brown, then turn over and brown the other side, about 2 minutes per side. Reduce the heat and remove the pork from the skillet. Add the garlic, celery and the remaining ½ teaspoon salt to the skillet and stir-fry for 30 seconds. Add the chicken stock and cook for 3 minutes (the celery should absorb the stock). Add the mushrooms and the remaining 1 tablespoon oil and stir-fry for 1 minute. Add the oyster sauce, pork and green onions and carefully stir for about 30 seconds. Dish out and serve immediately.

COOK'S NOTE
You can experiment with different kinds of mushrooms for this dish, and add other vegetables such as asparagus if you wish.

Stir-Fried Pork with Asian Eggplant

My mother used to grow Asian eggplant (also called Japanese eggplant) in our garden when we were growing up. These long, narrow eggplants are preferred for Chinese cooking because they have a firmer texture and fewer seeds than larger eggplants. This earthy, soul-satisfying dish—my friend Sabrina's favorite—gets a kick from the jalapeño peppers. Eggplant absorbs all of the seasonings around it like a sponge, so the morsels become little garlicky, spicy flavor bombs alongside the tender pieces of pork in this dish. Asian eggplant is available at Asian markets and some grocery stores. If you can't find Asian eggplant, you can use the more common type; just cut it into ½-inch (1.25-cm) cubes.

Serves 2 as a main dish with rice or 4 as part of a
*   multi-course meal*
Preparation time: 10 minutes + soaking time
Cooking time: 6 minutes

8 oz (250 g) pork loin or pork tenderloin, cut into ½-in
    (1.25-cm) pieces
¼ teaspoon plus 1 teaspoon salt, divided
Dash of white pepper
2 teaspoons all-purpose cornstarch
3 Asian eggplants, halved lengthwise and sliced
    diagonally into ½-in (1.25-cm) pieces
2 tablespoons brown bean paste
1 teaspoon sugar
1 teaspoon dry white wine
2 tablespoons oil
2 cloves garlic, minced
4 tablespoons chicken stock, homemade (page 62) or
    store-bought
2 medium jalapeño peppers, seeded and thinly sliced
2 green onions (scallions), cut into 1-in (2.5-cm) pieces

1 Toss the pork slices with ¼ teaspoon of the salt, the white pepper and the cornstarch. Cover and refrigerate 20 minutes.

2 Sprinkle the remaining 1 teaspoon salt over the eggplant and cover with cold water. Stir and let soak for 10 minutes. Drain and pat dry with paper towels.

3 In a small bowl, mix together the brown bean paste, sugar and white wine and set aside.

4 Heat the oil in a wok or skillet over high heat. Add the garlic, pork and eggplant and stir-fry for 3 minutes. Stir in the bean paste mixture, mix well and add the chicken stock. Stir-fry until the liquid is absorbed, about 2 minutes. Add the jalapeño peppers and green onions and stir-fry for 30 seconds. Dish out and serve immediately with steaming-hot rice.

COOK'S NOTE
You can use hoisin sauce in place of the brown bean paste; if you do so, reduce the sugar by half.

Seafood

I'm of Cantonese descent, but I'm not bragging when I say the Cantonese preparation of seafood is regarded as the finest and most inventive in all of China. Guangzhou (formerly known as Canton) is located along the southern coast of China, so seafood features prominently in its cuisine.

In China, seafood is mainly sold live in tanks. Many people go out on a daily basis to pick out a fresh whole fish to be steamed for dinner that night, or to buy a basketful of clams to be tossed in a pungent black bean sauce as soon as they get home. I remember shooting a Food Network special in Guangzhou with my mother. They had us pick out some live prawns from a market stall. We then walked across the street and handed them to a Chinese chef who tossed them in his wok with some garlic and green onions. Within minutes, we were sitting down to lunch. You can't get any fresher than that!

Many Chinese fish preparations are simple and elegant, letting the sweet and delicate flavor of the fish stand out. Fish is typically steamed with green onions, ginger and oil, as in the recipe for Braided Fish Steamed with Ginger and Green Onions (page 110) or Steamed Cantonese Whole Fish (page 119). Shrimp is always served at celebratory occasions in China, because the word for shrimp, *har*, sounds like laughter. I've included some of my favorite shrimp dishes from our family celebrations like the sweet, decadent Walnut Shrimp (page 114) and the healthy and light Jade Shrimp with Fragrant Vegetables (page 108).

Clams in Black Bean Sauce

This is an earthy dish; the pungent flavor of fermented black beans mingles with the briny taste of the clams, punctuated with ginger and dried chilies in a rich, savory sauce. I didn't appreciate this dish as a child, but when I went away for college my palate expanded (to also include coffee, clove cigarettes and red wine). In Boston, I got my weekly Clams in Black Bean Sauce fix at my favorite Chinatown dive, the Lucky Dragon. My mother always taught me to buy clams right before you cook them, but if you can't, keep them moist on ice in the fridge before cooking.

COOK'S NOTE
If any clams are open before cooking, tap the shell. If they don't close tightly, discard them.

Serves 4 as part of a multi-course meal
Preparation time: 15 minutes + soaking time
Cooking time: 8 minutes

2 tablespoons fermented black beans
1 tablespoon all-purpose cornstarch
1 teaspoon sugar
1 tablespoon water
36 littleneck clams
3 cups (750 ml) cold water
3 tablespoons white vinegar
1 cup (250 ml) boiling water
3 tablespoons oil
6 dried red chilies or chiles de árbol
2 teaspoons peeled and minced fresh ginger
2 cloves garlic, minced
1 green onion (scallion), finely chopped, for garnish

1 Place the black beans in a small bowl and cover with warm water. Stir for about 2 minutes to remove the excess salt. Remove the beans from the water, rinse and drain well.

2 Combine the cornstarch, sugar and 1 tablespoon water in a small bowl. Set aside.

3 Discard any broken or open clams and place the rest in a large bowl. Mix the 3 cups (750 ml) water with the vinegar and pour over the clams. Let stand 30 minutes.

4 Scrub the clams under running cold water, then place in a steamer over 1 cup (150 ml) boiling water. Steam for 5 minutes, or until clams open at least 1 inch (2.5 cm). Remove the clams as they open, discarding any that remain closed, and keep them warm. Strain the steaming liquid through double-thickness cheesecloth, reserving ½ cup (125 ml) of the liquid.

5 Heat the oil in a wok or skillet over medium-high heat. Add the strained black beans, chilies, garlic and ginger; stir-fry for 1 minute. Add the reserved steaming liquid and heat to boiling. Pour in the cornstarch mixture and stir for 1 minute or until the sauce thickens. Add the reserved clams and toss until nicely coated. Dish out and garnish with green onions. Serve immediately with steaming-hot rice.

Chinese Glazed Salmon

I'm always trying to get my kids to eat more fish for the omega-3 oils, but it isn't always easy. I was riffing on one of my mom's salmon recipes to make it more kid-friendly when my niece Griffin was visiting from Minneapolis. She took one bite and said, "OMG...salmon is my new jam." What I love about this recipe is that it's incredibly easy, and the marinade of soy sauce, ginger, lime juice, garlic and brown sugar makes it incredibly flavorful. My favorite part is the sweet, spicy and sticky glaze that's brushed over the salmon right before you serve it. When all the little kids saw Griffin devouring her salmon, they decided to try it, and before I knew it the entire platter was empty. My six year-old daughter Becca asked later, "Why does Griffin like salmon jam?"

Serves 6 as part of a multi-course meal
Preparation time: 10 minutes + marinating time
Cooking time: 14 minutes

MARINADE
½ cup (85 g) brown sugar
⅓ cup (80 ml) soy sauce
2 tablespoons hoisin sauce, homemade (page 25) or store-bought
2 tablespoons peeled and minced fresh ginger
⅛ teaspoon crushed red pepper
1 clove garlic, minced
1 tablespoon freshly squeezed lime juice
1 teaspoon dark sesame oil

1½ lbs (750 g) salmon fillet

1 Make the marinade: Whisk the marinade ingredients in a small bowl until blended. Pour half of the marinade over the salmon, turning the fillet over to coat thoroughly. Cover and refrigerate for 20 minutes.

2 Place the remaining marinade in a small saucepan over medium-high heat. Bring to a boil, then reduce heat to medium-low and simmer for about 14 minutes, or until the marinade forms a glaze.

3 Preheat broiler and place the marinated salmon on a broiler pan. Broil salmon until cooked through, about 8 minutes.

4 Remove salmon from the broiler. Transfer to a platter and brush the glaze over. Serve immediately with steaming-hot rice.

Shrimp with Lobster Sauce

"Hey, where's the lobster?" I've actually heard people say this at Chinese restaurants because the name of this dish is deceiving. There are no lobster tidbits in the sauce—the name simply means it contains the same flavorful pork, garlic and ginger sauce used in many Cantonese lobster dishes. This is an easy and tasty dish that is delicious served over rice. One of my husband Matthew's favorite memories from growing up in Schenectady, New York, was eating this dish on Sunday nights at Lum Fung's, his family's favorite Chinese restaurant.

Serves 2 as a main dish with rice or 4 as part of a multi-course meal
Preparation time: 12 minutes + marinating time
Cooking time: 4 minutes

8 oz (250 g) shelled and deveined medium-sized raw shrimp
½ teaspoon plus ½ tablespoon all-purpose cornstarch, divided
⅛ teaspoon salt
⅛ teaspoon dark sesame oil
6 tablespoons chicken stock, homemade (page 62) or store-bought, divided
½ teaspoon dark soy sauce
5 teaspoons oil, divided
4 oz (100 g) lean ground pork
1 clove garlic, minced
1 teaspoon peeled and minced fresh ginger
1 tablespoons dry white wine
1 egg, slightly beaten
1 green onion (scallion), finely chopped, for garnish

1 Follow the directions for "Eliminating Shrimp's 'Fishy' Taste" on page 20. (This step is optional.)

2 In a medium bowl, toss the shrimp with ½ teaspoon of the cornstarch, the salt and the sesame oil. Cover and refrigerate for 30 minutes.

3 Combine 2 tablespoons of the chicken stock, the remaining ½ tablespoon cornstarch and the soy sauce in a small bowl. Set aside.

4 Heat 2 teaspoons of the oil in a wok or skillet over medium-high heat. Add the shrimp and stir-fry 3 minutes or until pink. Remove the shrimp from the wok and set aside.

5 Heat the remaining 3 teaspoons of oil over medium-high heat. Add the pork, garlic and ginger and stir-fry for 2 minutes. Add the remaining 4 tablespoons chicken stock and the wine and heat to boiling. Gradually pour in the egg, stirring constantly, until it forms strands. Add the shrimp and stir-fry for 30 seconds. Dish out and garnish with green onions. Serve immediately with steaming-hot rice.

Lobster with Ginger and Scallions

This dish reminds me of all the Chinese banquets our parents would drag us to while we were growing up. It's a blur of round tables, "lazy Susans," lots of yelling in Chinese and the clinking of glasses. As kids, we did a lot of kicking each other under the table out of boredom until the food finally came—a glorious parade of celebratory dishes. We always hoped that Lobster with Ginger and Scallions would make an appearance, and if it did, we'd give each other a knowing smile that our patience was rewarded. In my mother's wonderful version of this recipe, whole lobster is boiled, then flash-fried and tossed in a delicious ginger and scallion sauce.

Serves 4 as part of a multi-course meal
Preparation time: 20 minutes
Cooking time: 8 minutes

½ teaspoon salt
¼ teaspoon white pepper
½ cup (65 g) plus 1 tablespoon all-purpose
   cornstarch, divided
1 tablespoon water
1 live lobster (about 2 lbs/1 kg)
Oil for frying
2 tablespoons oil
4 tablespoons peeled and minced fresh
   ginger
6 green onions (scallions); cut four of them
   into 1-in (2.5-cm) pieces, and trim and cut
   the other two into thin strips for garnish
1 cup (250 ml) chicken stock, homemade
   (page 62) or store-bought

COOK'S NOTE
You can actually deep-fry the
lobster in advance and freeze it.
When you want to serve it, simply
reheat the lobster in the oven,
prepare the sauce, and stir-fry
them together. You can also use
5 to 6 frozen lobster tails in place of
a whole lobster (ask the butcher to
chop each tail into 6 pieces).

1 Combine the salt, pepper and ½ cup (65 g) cornstarch in a bowl. In a separate bowl, combine the remaining 1 tablespoon cornstarch and 1 tablespoon water. Set aside.

2 Place the lobster in a large pot and cover with cold water (water should be 1 inch/2.5 cm above the lobster). Remove the lobster and bring the water to a boil. Submerge the lobster in the boiling water and cook for 3 minutes, then remove.

3 Twist off the head and cut off the end of the tail (clean the inside of the head and save it, along with the tail, for garnish). Twist off and discard the legs. Cutting through the shell, slice the tail in half lengthwise, then cut twice crosswise to make 6 pieces. Cut the claws in half or use a hammer to crack them open. The lobster meat should remain in the shells. Coat all exposed lobster meat, including the claws, with the dry cornstarch mixture.

4 Heat 3 to 4 inches (7.5 cm to 10 cm) of the oil in a wok or deep skillet to 350°F (175°C). Deep-fry the lobster for 1 minute, then transfer to a paper-towel-lined sheet pan to drain. Pour out the oil (discard or save for another time).

5 Wash and thoroughly dry the wok or skillet, then heat the 2 tablespoons oil over medium-high heat. Add the ginger, the 1-inch (2.5-cm) green onion pieces and the lobster. Stir-fry for 1 minute, then add the chicken stock and bring to a boil. Pour in the cornstarch and water mixture and continue stirring until the sauce thickens, about 30 seconds.

6 Place on a serving platter and garnish with the green onion strips. Place the cleaned lobster head at the top of the platter and the tail at the opposite end for garnish. Serve immediately with steaming-hot rice.

Jade Shrimp with Fragrant Vegetables

As mentioned previously, shrimp is often served at celebratory occasions in China. My mother would always serve a shrimp dish like Jade Shrimp with Fragrant Vegetables at birthday parties—and, as I recall, when my brother Billy finished his Ph.D. (My parents celebrated the Ph.D., but not the pierced ear he'd acquired while studying abroad!) Despite the ongoing culture clash in our home, we always found ourselves laughing at the dinner table. This easy and healthy dish is loaded with bright pink shrimp and toothsome snow peas and broccoli. The garlic infused in the sauce is what gives the vegetables their fabulous fragrance.

Serves 2 as a main dish with rice or 4 as part of a multi-course meal
Preparation time: 12 minutes + marinating time
Cooking time: 5 minutes

8 oz (250 g) shelled and deveined large-sized raw shrimp
2 teaspoons all-purpose cornstarch, divided
Dash of white pepper
¼ teaspoon dark sesame oil
8 oz (250 g) broccoli florets
2 oz (50 g) snow peas, tips and strings removed
1 tablespoon water
1 tablespoon oyster sauce
2 tablespoons oil, divided
1 clove garlic, minced
1 small white onion, thinly sliced
4 tablespoons chicken stock, homemade (page 62) or store-bought
2 oz (50 g) canned baby corn
⅛ teaspoon salt
2 tablespoons fresh coriander leaves (cilantro), for garnish

1 Follow directions for "Eliminating Shrimp's 'Fishy' Taste" on page 20. (This step is optional.)

2 In a medium bowl, toss the shrimp with 1 teaspoon of the cornstarch, the pepper and the sesame oil. Cover and refrigerate for 30 minutes.

3 Blanch the snow peas and broccoli florets in boiling water until tender, about 1 minute. Using a slotted spoon, transfer the vegetables to an ice water bath to cool, then drain and set aside.

4 In a small bowl, mix 1 tablespoon water, the remaining 1 tablespoon cornstarch and the oyster sauce. Set aside.

5 Heat 1 tablespoon of the oil in a wok or skillet over medium-high heat. Add the shrimp and stir-fry for 2 minutes, or until they turn pink. Remove from the pan and set aside.

6 Wash and thoroughly dry the wok or skillet, then heat the remaining 1 tablespoon oil over high heat. Add the garlic and onion and stir-fry until fragrant, about 1 minute. Pour in the chicken stock and heat to boiling. Cover and cook for 1 minute, then stir in the cornstarch mixture and cook until the sauce thickens, about 1 minute.

7 Add the baby corn and salt and stir-fry for 1 minute. Stir in the reserved shrimp, snow peas and broccoli and cook, stirring constantly for 1 minute, until the shrimp are hot. Dish out and garnish with the coriander leaves. Serve immediately with steaming-hot rice.

Braided Fish Steamed with Ginger and Green Onions

I remember the exact moment my mother and I got inspired to create this dish. We were visiting Seattle and walking around Pike Place Market when we spotted the most gorgeous salmon and halibut fillets. We were planning for a dinner party that night and wanted to serve both kinds of fish, but we weren't sure how. My niece Griffin walked by us with a long French braid, and we yelled out in unison, "I know! Let's braid the fish!" This dish is impressive to behold, and diners love the surprising "twist." The fish is marinated, steamed to perfection and topped with sizzling ginger oil and strands of green onion. The result is delicate, fragrant and flaky.

Serves 4 as part of a multi-course meal
Preparation time: 15 minutes + marinating time
Cooking Time: 15 to 20 minutes

3 teaspoons peeled and minced fresh ginger, divided
½ teaspoon salt
½ teaspoon sugar
5 tablespoons oil, divided
¼ teaspoon white pepper
1 clove garlic, minced
1 skinless salmon fillet (about 2 lbs/1 kg), cut into three long ¾-in (2-cm) wide strips (save the trimmings for another use)
1 skinless halibut fillet (about 2 lbs/1 kg), cut into two long ¾-in (2-cm) wide strips (save the trimmings for another use)
1 tablespoon all-purpose cornstarch
2 tablespoons soy sauce
2 green onions, trimmed and cut into thin strips, for garnish

1 In a small bowl, mix together 2 teaspoons of the ginger, the salt, the sugar, 1 tablespoon of the oil, the pepper and the garlic. Spread this mixture all over the fish. Cover and refrigerate for 30 minutes.

2 Sprinkle the cornstarch over the fish. Braid two strips of the salmon together with one strip of the halibut into a straight, long braid. You will need to cut the third strip of salmon in half and use about half of the second halibut strip to continue the braid. Tuck the connecting edges in as best you can so it looks like a continuous braid. Place on a heatproof platter and cover with plastic wrap for 10 minutes (or longer if refrigerated).

3 Place the plate of braided fish on a rack in a steamer. Cover and steam over boiling water until the fish flakes easily with a fork, 10 to 15 minutes.

4 In a small saucepan, heat the remaining 4 tablespoons of oil over medium-high heat. Add the remaining 1 teaspoon ginger. When the ginger sizzles, pour the oil over the fish. Pour the soy sauce over the fish and garnish with green onion.

COOK'S NOTE
If you can't find halibut fillets, substitute 2 fillets of orange roughy (about 1 to 1¼ lbs, or 500 to 600 g). For a simpler preparation, skip the braiding and steam as directed. Also, you can use a single kind of fish for this recipe, but it won't be as visually interesting.

Combine marinade ingredients and spread mixture over the fish. Cover and refrigerate.

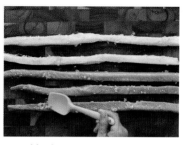

Sprinkle the cornstarch over the fish.

Lay down 2 strips of salmon and 1 strip of halibut.

Braid into a straight, long braid.

Tuck the connecting edges in. Place on a heat proof plate, cover with plastic wrap and allow to rest.

Place the plate in a steamer. Cover and steam over boiling water until the fish flakes easily.

Heat the remaining oil in a small saucepan. Add the ginger and once it sizzles, pour over the fish.

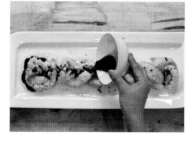

Pour the soy sauce over the fish and garnish with green onion.

Stir-Fried Fish Fillet and Chinese Broccoli

Our favorite Chinese restaurant in the San Fernando Valley is called Sam Woo. It has roast Chinese ducks and sides of roast pig hanging in the window, and of course it's cash only. The place is always packed with Chinese families devouring their eight-course meals, because it's the best Cantonese food in the neighborhood. I took my mom there with the twins a few years ago and we ordered a fish fillet with Chinese broccoli dish. The velvety gravy made this dish so tasty that the twins gobbled up every bite of the fish *and* the Chinese broccoli. It inspired me to create my own version; I hope it gets your kids to eat their broccoli, too!

Serves 2 as a main dish with rice or 4 as part of a multi-course meal
Preparation time: 15 minutes + marinating time
Cooking time: 10 minutes

1 teaspoon Chinese rice wine or sherry
2½ teaspoons all-purpose cornstarch, divided
½ teaspoon dark sesame oil
1 egg white
½ teaspoon salt
Dash of white pepper
12 oz (350 g) boneless fish fillets (mild white fish, such as tilapia, cod or orange roughy), cut into 1½ x ½-in (3.75 x 1.25-cm) pieces
½ teaspoon soy sauce
1 teaspoon oyster sauce
½ teaspoon sugar
1 tablespoon water
½ teaspoon dark sesame oil
1 bunch Chinese broccoli (about 1 lb/500 g), ends trimmed
2 tablespoons oil, divided
1 clove garlic, minced
1 tablespoon peeled and minced fresh ginger, cut into matchsticks
½ cup (125 ml) fish stock, homemade (page 62) or store-bought

1 Mix the rice wine or sherry with 1 teaspoon of the cornstarch, the sesame oil, egg white, salt and pepper in a medium bowl until blended. Add the fish pieces and toss to coat. Cover and refrigerate 20 minutes.

2 In a small bowl, combine the soy sauce, oyster sauce, the remaining 1½ teaspoons cornstarch, sugar, water and sesame oil until blended. Set aside.

3 Blanch the Chinese broccoli in boiling water until tender, about 2 minutes. Using a slotted spoon, transfer to an ice water bath to cool. Drain and cut into 2-inch (5-cm) pieces.

4 Heat 1 tablespoon of the oil in a wok or skillet over medium-high heat. Add the fish and stir-fry until lightly browned. Stir gently so as not to break up the pieces. Remove the fish from the pan and set aside.

5 Wash and thoroughly dry the wok or skillet, then heat the remaining 1 tablespoon oil over medium-high heat. Add the garlic and ginger and stir-fry until fragrant, about 1 minute. Stir in the Chinese broccoli and stir-fry for 1 minute more, then add the reserved fish and stir-fry gently for 1 minute.

6 Pour in the fish stock and bring to a boil. Add the cornstarch mixture and stir-fry until sauce is thickened and all ingredients are nicely coated, about 2 minutes. Dish out and serve immediately with steaming-hot rice.

Chinese-Style Parchment Fish

Wait a minute, Mr. Postman. These bundles of fish—topped with a classic Cantonese sauce of rice wine, soy sauce, rice vinegar, sesame oil and ginger—are baked to perfection in a paper package that, once opened, releases an intoxicating aroma. The fish inside is flaky, delicate and flavorful. None of your guests will want to return this dish to sender! When I swap out the soy sauce for tamari, it's my girlfriend Jeannie Mai's favorite dish, because it's healthy, fresh and totally gluten-free.

Serves 4 as part of a multi-course meal
Preparation time: 20 minutes
Cooking time: 15 minutes

4 heads baby bok choy, sliced in half
    lengthwise
1 small red bell pepper, thinly sliced
Four 6-oz (175-g) halibut, orange roughy
    or red snapper fillets
½ teaspoon white pepper
2 green onions (scallions), cut into 1-in
    (2.5-cm) pieces
Zest from ½ orange, cut into slivers
3 tablespoons soy sauce
1 teaspoon Chinese rice wine or sherry
1½ teaspoons unseasoned rice vinegar
1½ teaspoons dark sesame oil
2 teaspoons peeled and minced fresh
    ginger
¼ teaspoon salt
⅛ teaspoon white pepper

1 Preheat oven to 400°F (200°C).

2 Tear off four large squares of parchment paper and arrange on two sheet pans.

3 Distribute the bok choy, flat side down, and bell pepper evenly among the squares. Place one halibut fillet on top of the vegetables in each square, sprinkle with white pepper and top with the green onions and orange zest.

4 In a small bowl, combine the soy sauce, rice wine, vinegar, sesame oil and ginger. Spoon the mixture evenly over the fish fillets. Season with the salt and pepper.

5 Fold the parchment paper tightly around the edges in ¼-inch (6-mm) folds to create a half-moon shape. Make sure you press as you crimp and fold to seal the packets well. Bake for 15 minutes.

6 Transfer each packet to a plate. Give each diner a knife to slit open their packet, and warn them to be careful of the steam that will escape. Serve immediately with steaming-hot rice.

Walnut Shrimp

When I think of Hong Kong cuisine, I always think of Walnut Shrimp, which is a Hong Kong sensation. Fusion dishes like this, which incorporates mayonnaise and condensed milk, are a hallmark of the inventiveness of Hong Kong chefs. When my mother made this for me for the first time, I couldn't believe this combination would work, but boy, was I wrong! It's decadent and creamy, with a pop of brightness from the fresh lemon and lime juice. Tossed with crispy shrimp and candied walnuts, it's an indulgent dish that I make for dinner parties and special occasions, or anytime I feel like treating myself.

Serves 4 as part of a multi-course meal
Preparation time: 10 minutes
Cooking time: 5 minutes

8 oz (250 g) shelled and deveined large-sized raw shrimp
1 tablespoon egg white
1 tablespoon all-purpose cornstarch
Dash baking soda
Dash garlic salt
½ teaspoon oil

DRESSING
4 tablespoons sweetened condensed milk
4 tablespoons mayonnaise
1 teaspoon freshly squeezed lemon juice
1 teaspoon freshly squeezed lime juice

Oil for frying
4 tablespoons store-bought candied walnuts

1 Follow the directions for "Eliminating Shrimp's 'Fishy' Taste" on page 20. (This step is optional.)

2 In a small bowl, mix together the egg white, cornstarch, baking soda, garlic salt and ½ teaspoon oil to form a smooth paste. Add the shrimp and blend to coat very well.

3 In a medium bowl, combine the sweetened condensed milk, mayonnaise and lemon and lime juices. Beat until smooth, then set aside.

4 In a wok or deep skillet, heat 2 to 3 inches (5 to 7.5 cm) of oil to 350°F (175°C). Fry the shrimp until light brown, 3 to 4 minutes, turning as necessary. Remove from the oil and transfer to a paper-towel-lined sheet pan. Increase the oil temperature to 375°F (190°C). Fry the shrimp again for 1 more minute, then transfer to a paper towel-lined sheet pan and drain well.

5 Add the shrimp to the mayonnaise mixture and stir until well covered. Transfer to a serving dish, sprinkle the candied walnuts on top and serve immediately with steaming-hot rice.

Sesame Scallops

Whenever my mother's buffet restaurant put these Sesame Scallops on the menu, a line would immediately form an hour before opening. I was the coat-check girl (I made a lot of tips from those heavy coats during Minnesota winters!), and I would watch in amazement as customers piled their plates high with this dish. The tender scallops are dipped in a light batter, flash-fried and then tossed in a heavenly hot-and-sour glaze. The scallops are then surrounded by a ring of light, crunchy rice noodles and garnished with sesame seeds. According to a Chinese saying, sesame seeds improve the spirits. I can guarantee you that these scallops will put you in a fantastic mood.

12 oz (350 g) fresh sea scallops
2 tablespoons oil
1 teaspoon soy sauce
¼ teaspoon salt
¼ teaspoon dark sesame oil
Dash of white pepper

SAUCE
½ cup (125 ml) water
4 tablespoons all-purpose cornstarch
1 cup (200 g) sugar
1 cup (250 ml) chicken stock, homemade
   (page 62) or store-bought
¾ cup (185 ml) white vinegar
2 teaspoons dark soy sauce
2 teaspoons chili paste, homemade
   (page 25) or store-bought
1 teaspoon oil
1 clove garlic, finely chopped

BATTER
½ cup (65 g) all-purpose flour
½ cup (125 ml) water
4 tablespoons all-purpose cornstarch
1 tablespoon oil
1 teaspoon baking soda
½ teaspoon salt

Oil for frying
2 oz (50 g) dried rice stick noodles
2 tablespoons toasted sesame seeds

Serves 4 to 6 as part of a multi-course meal
Preparation time: 30 minutes
Cooking time: 30 minutes

1 Toss the scallops with the 2 tablespoons oil, soy sauce, ¼ teaspoon salt, sesame oil and white pepper. Cover and refrigerate for 20 minutes.

2 Make the sauce: Combine the water and 4 tablespoons cornstarch in a small bowl. Bring the sugar, chicken stock, vinegar, soy sauce, chili paste, 1 teaspoon oil and garlic to a boil. Stir in the cornstarch mixture and cook, stirring constantly, until the sauce thickens. Remove from heat.

3 Make the batter: Combine all batter ingredients and mix until blended. Stir the scallops into the batter to coat well.

4 In a wok or deep skillet, heat 2 to 3 inches (5 to 7.5 cm) of oil to 350°F (175°C). Pull noodles apart gently. Divide the noodles into four batches and fry one batch at a time for 5 seconds, or until puffed, turning once. Drain on a paper-towel-lined sheet pan.

5 Fry about 15 scallops at a time, turning occasionally, until light brown, about 2 minutes. Drain on a paper-towel-lined sheet pan. Increase oil temperature to 375°F (175°C) and re-fry all
the scallops at once until golden brown, about 1 minute. Return to the sheet pan to drain.

6 Reheat the sauce. Transfer the scallops to a platter and pour the sauce over, then sprinkle with toasted sesame seeds. Arrange the fried noodles around scallops. Serve immediately with steaming-hot rice.

Crispy Fish with Ginger-Scallion Sauce

My mother always prepared Crispy Fish with Ginger-Scallion Sauce on the day of the Chinese New Year. The Chinese word for fish, *yu*, sounds the same as the word for abundance, so we eat this for good luck and prosperity. When my mother and I made this dish on our PBS Show, I talked about this symbolism, as well as that of the lotus root, which represents fertility. My mother's on-camera response to me was, "You better hurry up," a not-so subtle way of letting me know she wanted more grandkids, and soon. (I did take her advice—the twins were born a couple years later!) In this dish, the entire fish is marinated in sesame oil and then flash-fried in a smooth batter, resulting in a supremely tender and flaky fish. Topped with a sizzling ginger-scallion sauce, it's delicious any time of year.

Serves 4 as part of a multi-course meal
Preparation time: 30 minutes
Cooking time: 15 minutes

GINGER-SCALLION SAUCE
2 tablespoons oil
2 teaspoons peeled and minced fresh
    ginger
2 cloves garlic, minced
½ cup (125 ml) chicken stock, homemade
    (page 62) or store-bought
4 tablespoons white vinegar
4 tablespoons soy sauce
1 tablespoon sugar
1 finely chopped green onion (scallion)

1½ lbs (750 g) whole tilapia, catfish or red
    snapper, well cleaned
2⅛ teaspoons salt, divided
2 teaspoons peeled and minced fresh
    ginger
⅛ teaspoon sugar
2 teaspoons dark sesame oil
2 green onions (scallions), cut into 2-in
    (5-cm) pieces
4 tablespoons all-purpose flour
2 tablespoons all-purpose cornstarch
¼ teaspoon baking soda
4 tablespoons water
½ tablespoon oil
Oil for frying

1 Make the sauce: Heat 2 tablespoons of oil in a small saucepan over medium-high heat. Add the ginger and the garlic and stir-fry for 1 minute. Add the chicken stock, vinegar, soy sauce and sugar and bring to a boil. Remove from the heat and allow to cool.

2 Make 3 cuts across the fish, almost down to the bone. In a small bowl, combine 2 teaspoons of the salt with the ginger, sugar and sesame oil and rub the inside and outside of the fish. Marinate for 20 minutes (if longer, cover and refrigerate). Stuff the fish cavity with the green onion pieces and place on a platter.

3 In a small bowl, combine the flour, cornstarch, baking soda, water, oil and the remaining ⅛ teaspoon salt. Mix into a smooth batter and brush over the fish.

4 Heat 2 to 3 inches (5 to 7.5 cm) of the oil in a wok or pot to 350°F (175°C). Deep-fry the fish for 6 to 7 minutes, then turn it over and fry for another 6 to 7 minutes, or until golden brown. Drain well on a paper-towel-lined sheet pan. Transfer to a platter. Serve with the ginger-scallion sauce on the side. Add the chopped green onions to the sauce just before serving.

Make 3 cuts across the fish. Rub the inside and outside of the fish with the marinade.

Stuff the fish cavity with the sliced green onions.

Combine the batter ingredients and brush over the fish.

Deep-fry the fish for 6 to 7 minutes. Drain well on a paper towel-lined sheet pan.

Tea-Smoked Sea Bass

My friend Lisa Boalt Richardson is a tea expert and the author of numerous books on tea. She was fascinated when I told her about my mother's technique for tea-smoking sea bass, and sent me a tin of her favorite jasmine tea to use in this recipe. The technique used here allows you to create an authentic smoky Asian flavor in a conventional oven. After the fish is marinated, it's smoked in the oven over a mixture of brown sugar, tea leaves and rice. The smoking effect is incredible, as every flaky and delicate bite is imbued with sweet and smoky jasmine tea flavor.

Serves 6 as part of a multi-course meal
Preparation time: 15 minutes + soaking and marinating time
Cooking time: 15 minutes

1½ lbs (750 g) skinless sea bass fillets, cut into 4 or 5 pieces total
1½ teaspoons salt, divided
1 teaspoon peeled and minced fresh ginger
1 tablespoon oil
⅛ teaspoon white pepper
2 teaspoons soy sauce
1 tablespoon white vinegar
2 teaspoons sugar
2 teaspoons dark sesame oil
1 English cucumber, cut into very thin slices
2 tablespoons oolong or jasmine tea leaves
1 cup (200 g) brown sugar
4 tablespoons uncooked rice

1 Wipe the sea bass pieces dry with paper towel.

2 Make the marinade: In a small bowl, combine 1 teaspoon of the salt with the ginger, oil, pepper and soy sauce. Rub all sides of the fish with the marinade and place in the refrigerator for 30 minutes or longer.

3 Preheat oven to 500°F (260°C).

4 In a medium bowl, blend the vinegar, sugar, sesame oil and the remaining ½ teaspoon salt. Add the cucumber and toss. Let stand for 10 minutes. Discard the excess dressing and place the cucumber slices in an overlapping pattern around the edge of a serving platter.

5 Completely line the inside surface of a large covered Dutch oven or wok with heavy foil. Combine the tea leaves, brown sugar and rice in the foil-lined pan and spread out evenly. Place a metal steam rack in the pan, making sure it stands at least 1 inch (2.5 cm) above the tea leaves. Place the marinated fish on the rack.

6 Cover the pan tightly—this is important, because the smoke must be contained in the pan for the fish to smoke properly. Place in the preheated oven and bake for 15 minutes. Remove from the oven and let sit, covered, for 5 minutes. Carefully open the lid. Using a spatula, carefully transfer the fish to the cucumber-lined platter. Serve immediately with steaming-hot rice.

COOK'S NOTE
If your pan cover doesn't fit tightly enough, place foil around the outside of the cover and pan so the smoke doesn't escape.

Steamed Cantonese Whole Fish

When I taught a class at the Gourmandise School in Santa Monica recently, I decided to teach my students how to make my mother's Steamed Cantonese Whole Fish recipe. Whole sea bass or red snapper is marinated in fermented black beans and classic Chinese seasonings and then steamed to perfection. Steaming is the purest way to cook fresh fish—and after making it, you'll see why. It turns out tender and flaky, and the sweet and delicate flavor of the fish shines through. In fact, one student declared, "That is the best fish I've ever eaten!" The key is timing. You don't want to overcook it, so be sure you have your timer close by.

Serves 4 as part of a multi-course meal
Preparation time: 10 minutes + soaking
*   and marinating time*
Cooking time: 10 minutes

2 tablespoons fermented black beans
2 green onions (scallions), trimmed and cut
    into thin strips, divided
1½ lbs (750 g) whole sea bass, striped bass,
    or red snapper, well cleaned
1 teaspoon peeled and minced fresh ginger
4 tablespoons oil, divided
1 clove garlic, minced
½ teaspoon salt
¼ teaspoon sugar
1 teaspoon soy sauce
¼ teaspoon dark sesame oil
One 2-in (5-cm) piece fresh ginger, peeled
    and slivered

1 Place the black beans in a small bowl and cover with warm water. Stir for about 2 minutes to remove the excess salt. Remove the beans from the water, rinse and drain well.

2 Place the green onions strips in a bowl with ice water to cover. Let stand 10 minutes, or until the strips curl.

3 Slash the fish crosswise 3 times on each side. In a small bowl, mix the ginger, 2 tablespoons of the oil, the drained black beans, and the garlic, salt, sugar, soy sauce and sesame oil. Rub the cavity and outside of the fish with the mixture. Cover and refrigerate for 30 minutes or longer.

4 Place the fish on a heatproof plate. Place the plate on a rack in a steamer, cover and steam over boiling water until the fish flakes easily with a fork, about 10 minutes. (Add more boiling water if necessary.)

5 In a small saucepan, heat the remaining 2 tablespoons oil over medium-high heat until it smokes. Add the ginger slivers and half of the green onions. Pour the hot oil over the fish (you'll hear sizzling).

6 Garnish with the remaining green onions. Serve immediately with steaming-hot rice.

COOK'S NOTE
This dish can be cooked in the microwave. Place the fish on a microwave-safe plate, cover with plastic wrap and cook for 3 minutes on high. Let stand for 2 minutes, then rotate the dish and cook on high for an additional 2 minutes.

Vegetables and Tofu

Vegetable and tofu dishes are always included as part of a multi-course meal on a Chinese dinner table. Vegetable dishes are often the cooling yin counterpoint to spicy yang meat dishes or deep-fried foods. Chinese cuisine boasts an array of vegetable and tofu dishes, many stemming from the Buddhist tradition of a strictly vegetarian diet such as Harvest Delight (page 124), which is gorgeous in its simplicity and in its presentation.

I love to create interesting textures in my vegetable dishes. JJ's Spicy-Crispy Tofu with Green Beans, for example, (page 131) contains cubes of tofu that are flash-fried to crunchy perfection on the outside with a soft pillowy center, then tossed with crisp green beans in a spicy sauce.

Just because it's a vegetable dish doesn't mean it has to be plain or predictable. The kick of the crushed red pepper in the Sichuan Tofu with Broccoli recipe (page 126), or the garlic, nutty sesame oil and rich oyster sauce of Spicy-Garlicky Asian Eggplant (page 127) add excitement to rival any meat-based dish.

When you're looking for a simple vegetable side dish to round out your Chinese dinner menu, I recommend the Asparagus with Wild Mushrooms (page 122) and the Stir-Fried Kale and Broccoli (page 125). Both are straightforward to prepare, yet incredibly flavorful, light and healthy. Feel free to improvise and experiment with these recipes using a combination of your favorite veggies.

Asparagus with Wild Mushrooms

Years ago, my mother was living with me in a tiny guest house in Laurel Canyon. We had to ask our neighbors, Patrick and Peter, to store a hundred pounds of meat and shrimp in their extra freezer, because our freezer couldn't accommodate it. We were testing recipes all the time and needed the inventory handy. The other neighbors would give us funny looks as we were crossing the cul-de-sac with yet another frozen block of shrimp. Anyway, we brought dinner over to Patrick and Peter's house as a thank-you gesture. They love veggies, so we grilled up some fish along with this easy and healthy stir-fry, which is loaded with tender, crisp asparagus and aromatic wild mushrooms in an oyster-sauce glaze. Luckily, I have two huge freezers now, but I'm sure I still have a pound or two of chicken breasts at Patrick and Peter's house!

Serves 4 as part of a multi-course meal
Preparation time: 5 minutes
Cooking time: 3 minutes

2 teaspoons all-purpose cornstarch
2 teaspoons cold water
1 tablespoon oil
2 cloves garlic, minced
1 lb (500 g) asparagus, ends trimmed
½ teaspoon salt
4 oz (100 g) fresh shiitake or oyster mushrooms, stemmed and thinly sliced
1 tablespoon oyster sauce
½ cup (125 ml) chicken stock, homemade (page 62) or store-bought

COOK'S NOTE
This recipe would be great with any variety of mushrooms. You can also increase the amount. If the mushrooms are very large, be sure to cut them into smaller pieces.

1 In a small bowl, mix together the cornstarch and cold water.

2 Heat the oil in a wok or skillet over medium-high heat. Add the garlic, asparagus and salt and stir-fry for 1 minute. Add the mushrooms and continue to stir-fry until mixed. Stir in the oyster sauce and chicken stock and heat to boiling. Pour in the cornstarch mixture and continue to cook, stirring constantly, until the sauce thickens and all ingredients are nicely coated, about 30 seconds. Turn off the heat and remove the asparagus with tongs. Arrange the asparagus across a platter and top with the mushrooms. Serve immediately with steaming-hot rice.

Chinese Long Beans with Cashews

My mother grew Chinese long beans in our garden during the summer. As a kid, I always thought they looked like some kind of vegetation from outer space, being so long (the average length is 1 to 1½ feet, or up to 45 cm) and skinny, with rather wrinkly skin. When you bite into these beans, though, you'll understand why they belong on earth. Although the flavor is similar to green beans, they have a distinct tight yet juicy texture. When they're stir-fried in oil with aromatics, they soak up the flavors without getting soggy. Paired with sweet, crunchy cashews and classic Chinese flavors, this recipe is a healthy family favorite.

Serves 4 as part of a multi-course meal
Preparation time: 5 minutes
Cooking time: 3 minutes

1 lb (500 g) Chinese long beans, trimmed and cut into 2-in (5-cm) pieces
2 tablespoons oil
2 cloves garlic, minced
2 tablespoons hoisin sauce, homemade (page 25) or store-bought
2 tablespoons oyster sauce
2 oz (50 g) roasted cashews

1 Blanch the long beans in boiling water until tender-crisp, about 2 minutes. Transfer the beans to an ice water bath with a slotted spoon to cool, then drain and set aside.

2 Heat the oil in a wok or skillet over medium-high heat. Add the long beans and stir-fry for 2 minutes. Add the garlic, hoisin sauce and oyster sauce and stir-fry for another 30 seconds.

3 Dish out and garnish with roasted cashews. Serve immediately with steaming-hot rice.

COOK'S NOTE
You may substitute green beans for the long beans, but blanch them for 5 minutes instead of 2 minutes.

Harvest Delight

In early fall, Chinese people celebrate the gathering of the harvest during the Autumn Moon Festival. Families come together and eat round-shaped foods, like moon cakes, to symbolize familial harmony and unity. This Harvest Delight vegetable dish is something my mother would serve as part of our Autumn Moon Festival banquet. This is a simple, pure and clean dish that honors the vegetables with its beautiful plating. Because it's so easy and healthy, I now make it year-round.

Serves 4 as part of a multi-course meal
Preparation time: 6 minutes
Cooking time: 6 minutes

8 oz (250 g) bok choy, trimmed and cut
    diagonally into ½-in (1.25-cm) slices
1 red bell pepper, thinly sliced
4 oz (100 g) snow peas, tips and strings removed
5 teaspoons oil, divided
1 teaspoon salt, divided
1 clove garlic, minced

1 Heat 2 teaspoons of the oil in wok or a skillet over medium-high heat. Add the bok choy, ½ teaspoon of the salt and the garlic and stir-fry for 3 minutes. Remove the bok choy and place in the center of a serving platter in a long row, with the slices overlapping.

2 Clean and thoroughly dry the wok or skillet, then heat 2 more teaspoons oil over medium-high heat. Add the bell pepper and the remaining ½ teaspoon salt and stir-fry for 2 minutes. Remove the peppers from the wok and place at the top of the serving platter, above the bok choy.

3 Add 2 cups (500 ml) water to the wok or skillet and bring to a boil. Add the snow peas and cook over high heat until the water returns to boiling. Add the remaining 1 teaspoon oil and cook for 30 seconds more. Drain the snow peas and place at the bottom of the serving platter. Serve immediately alongside steaming-hot rice.

Stir-Fried Kale and Broccoli

In case you didn't get the memo, kale is taking the world by storm as one of the healthiest, most nutrient-dense foods on the planet. Loaded with Vitamins A, K and C, it also contains tons of minerals, anti-oxidants and omega-3s. My brother-in-law David is a huge fan of kale and was looking for new ways to prepare it, so I suggested this simple recipe. It's a classic Chinese vegetable stir-fry preparation with kale as a wonderful complement. Here's to your health—enjoy!

Serves 4 as part of a multi-course meal
Preparation time: 10 minutes
Cooking time: 4 minutes

4 cups (200 g) curly kale, stemmed and torn into chunks
2 cups (350 g) broccoli florets
2 teaspoons all-purpose cornstarch
2 teaspoons cold water
1 tablespoon soy sauce
1 teaspoon dark sesame oil
¼ teaspoon sugar
1 tablespoon Chinese rice wine or sherry
1 tablespoon oil
3 cloves garlic, minced
1 tablespoon peeled and minced fresh ginger
1 small red bell pepper, thinly sliced
1 small yellow bell pepper, thinly sliced
½ teaspoon salt
½ cup (125 ml) vegetable stock or chicken stock, homemade (page 62) or store-bought

1 Blanch the kale and broccoli in boiling water until bright green, about 1 minute. Using a slotted spoon, transfer to an ice water bath to cool, then drain and set aside.

2 Mix together the cornstarch and 2 teaspoons cold water in a small bowl. Set aside.

3 In a separate bowl, combine the soy sauce, sesame oil, sugar and rice wine or sherry and whisk to blend. Set aside.

4 Heat 1 tablespoon of oil over medium-high heat in a wok or skillet. Add the garlic and ginger and stir-fry until fragrant, about 30 seconds. Add the red and yellow bell pepper and stir-fry for 1 minute. Add the drained kale and broccoli and the salt; stir-fry for 30 seconds. Pour in the soy sauce mixture and stir-fry for 30 seconds.

5 Add the vegetable or chicken stock and heat to boiling, then pour in the cornstarch mixture. Continue to cook, stirring constantly, until the sauce thickens, about 30 seconds. Dish out and serve immediately with steaming-hot rice.

Sichuan Tofu with Broccoli

My friend Mary was trying to do Meatless Mondays, but she found it a struggle. "Okay," she told me, "this is getting really boring. I don't know what else to do with tofu. I have a block of it staring at me from my counter. Help!" Well, I'm here to say that tofu doesn't have to be boring; in fact, it can be scintillating, sexy, spicy and sublime! As my mother taught me, tofu soaks up all of the flavors around it. As long as you've got the right stuff—like the garlic, ginger, rice wine, soy sauce, oyster sauce and crushed red pepper in this recipe—your tofu will come alive and knock your socks off.

Serves 4 as part of a multi-course meal
Preparation time: 5 minutes
Cooking time: 10 minutes

4 cups (700 g) broccoli florets
2 tablespoons oil, divided
One 16-oz (500-g) block firm tofu, drained, patted dry and cut into cubes
2 cloves garlic, minced
1 tablespoon peeled and minced fresh ginger
1 tablespoon Chinese rice wine or sherry
2 tablespoons soy sauce
1 tablespoon oyster sauce
½ teaspoon crushed red pepper

1 Blanch the broccoli in boiling water until tender-crisp, about 1 minute. Using a slotted spoon, transfer to an ice water bath to cool, then drain and set aside.

2 Heat 1 tablespoon of the oil in the wok or skillet over medium-high heat. Add the tofu pieces and fry until brown, about 2 minutes. Turn the pieces over and cook for about 3 more minutes. Remove from the pan and set aside.

3 Heat the remaining 1 tablespoon oil in the wok or skillet over medium-high heat. Add the garlic and ginger and stir-fry until fragrant, about 30 seconds. Add the broccoli and stir-fry for 1 minute. Add the reserved tofu, rice wine or sherry, soy sauce, oyster sauce and crushed red pepper; stir-fry for 2 minutes. Dish out and serve immediately with steaming-hot rice.

Spicy-Garlicky Asian Eggplant

Asian eggplants are long and narrow in shape, with thinner skin and a sweeter taste than larger American eggplants. They absorb all the flavors around them, so if you love garlic you'll love this recipe. The eggplant is soaked in salt water to remove the bitter taste; this also makes it absorb less oil when it's cooked. I was planning to cook this for my husband when we were first dating, but my mother said, "Will he want to kiss you after all that garlic?" I decided to wait and save this recipe for our six-month anniversary.

Serves 4 as part of a multi-course meal
Preparation time: 5 minutes + soaking time
Cooking time: 5 minutes

4 Asian eggplants, cut in half lengthwise then
    diagonally into ½-in (1.25-cm) slices
2 teaspoons salt
1 tablespoon oyster sauce
1 teaspoon sugar
1 teaspoon dark sesame oil
2 tablespoons oil
2 cloves garlic, minced
2 hot red chili peppers, seeded and thinly
    sliced
2 tablespoons water

1 Cover the eggplants with water. Add the salt and stir to dissolve. Let stand for 5 minutes, then drain well.

2 Mix together the oyster sauce, sugar and sesame oil in a small bowl. Set aside.

3 Heat the oil in a wok or skillet over medium-high heat. Add the garlic, chili peppers and eggplant and stir-fry for 2 minutes. Add the 2 tablespoons water and continue stir-frying for 2 more minutes. Pour in the oyster sauce mixture and stir well to mix. Dish out and serve immediately with steaming-hot rice.

COOK'S NOTE
Asian eggplant (also known as Japanese eggplant) is available at many Asian markets. You can substitute regular eggplant; just cut it lengthwise into 4 to 6 strips before slicing.

Stir-Fried Spinach with Garlic

When my friend Rita was pregnant with her son Baby Dasch (we still call him that even though he's four years old now), her doctor said she needed more folic acid. She got tired of spinach salads, spinach quiche and spinach kale smoothies pretty fast, so my mom recommended I make this quick and easy spinach stir-fry dish for her. Rita loved it so much that she made me cook her two more servings on the spot. Lightly seasoned with a bit of shallot and garlic and tossed with a bit of oyster sauce, this is a simple, healthy and delicious way to cook spinach.

Serves 4 as part of a multi-course meal
Preparation time: 5 minutes
Cooking time: 3 minutes

1 tablespoon oil
1 teaspoon minced shallot
1 teaspoon peeled and minced fresh
   ginger
12 oz (350 g) spinach leaves, trimmed and
   cleaned
½ teaspoon salt
2 teaspoons oyster sauce

Heat the oil in a wok or skillet over medium-high heat. Add the shallot and ginger and stir-fry until fragrant, about 30 seconds. Add the spinach and salt and stir-fry until wilted, about 1 minute, then add the oyster and stir-fry for 1 minute more. Dish out and serve immediately with steaming-hot rice.

Baby Bok Choy with Ginger and Garlic

This dish is so fast, my stepdaughter Kyla wanted to call it Quick-Time Baby Bok Choy with Ginger and Garlic (this was during her "Quick-Time" phase: Quick-Time Pancakes, Quick-Time Pizza, Quick-Time Nap—you get the picture). It's a great recipe for a busy weeknight because it's super duper fast and easy, but it's also very flavorful and nutrient-rich, thanks to the baby bok choy. Why not make this in the same time it takes to steam the same old baby carrots or green beans? It's sure to garner a Quick-Time thank you from your family.

Serves 4 as part of a multi-course meal
Preparation time: 8 minutes
Cooking time: 3 minutes

1½ tablespoons oil
2 cloves garlic, minced
2 teaspoons peeled and minced fresh ginger
4 heads baby bok choy, cut in half lengthwise, then crosswise into small pieces
2 tablespoons soy sauce
½ teaspoon dark sesame oil
½ teaspoon salt
1 teaspoon sugar

Heat the oil in the wok or skillet over medium-high heat. Add the garlic and ginger and stir-fry until fragrant, about 30 seconds. Add the bok choy and stir-fry for 1 minute. Stir in the soy sauce, sesame oil, salt and sugar; stir-fry for 1 minute. Dish out and serve immediately with steaming-hot rice.

Eight-Vegetable Tofu

While one is the loneliest number that you'll ever do, eight is the luckiest number in all of China. The reason the number eight is considered lucky is because in Chinese the sound of the word eight (*ba*) is similar to the sound for the word "prosperity" (*fa*). That's why the Beijing Olympics began on 08/08/08. Get it? My mother and I came up with this colorful and healthy dish celebrating the number eight to bring good luck, joy and harmony to your dinner table. Filled with soy protein and oodles of fresh veggies, this is a gorgeous and nourishing one-pot dish.

Serves 4 as part of a multi-course meal
Preparation time: 30 minutes
Cooking time: 10 minutes

2 oz (50 g) snow peas, tips and strings removed, cut on the diagonal into 1-in (2.5-cm) pieces
2 oz (50 g) broccoli florets
2 teaspoons all-purpose cornstarch
2 teaspoons cold water
2 tablespoons oil, divided
One 16-oz (500-g) block firm tofu, drained, patted dry and cut into cubes
2 cloves garlic, minced
1 teaspoon peeled and minced fresh ginger
2 oz (50 g) sliced carrots
4 asparagus spears, trimmed and thinly sliced diagonally
2 oz (50 g) stemmed and sliced fresh mushrooms
2 oz (50 g) thinly sliced red bell pepper
4 heads baby bok choy, quartered lengthwise
2 oz (50 g) canned baby corn, drained, rinsed and sliced lengthwise
½ teaspoon salt
⅛ teaspoon white pepper
2 tablespoons oyster sauce
½ cup (125 ml) chicken stock, homemade (page 62) or store-bought

1 Blanch the snow peas and broccoli in boiling water until tender-crisp, about 1 minute. Using a slotted spoon, transfer the broccoli to an ice water bath to cool, then drain and set aside.

2 In a small bowl, mix together the cornstarch and 2 teaspoons cold water. Set aside.

3 Heat 1 tablespoon of the oil in a wok or skillet over medium-high heat. Add the tofu pieces and fry until brown, about 2 minutes. Flip the pieces over and fry for about 2 more minutes, then remove from the pan and set aside.

4 Heat the remaining tablespoon of oil over medium-high heat in a wok or skillet. Add the garlic and ginger and stir-fry until fragrant, about 30 seconds. Stir in the carrot, asparagus and mushrooms and stir-fry for 3 minutes. Add the red bell pepper and bok choy and stir-fry for 1 minute. Mix in the reserved snow peas, broccoli, baby corn, salt and white pepper; stir-fry for 1 minute. Add the reserved tofu and oyster sauce and gently stir-fry for 30 seconds more.

5 Pour in the chicken stock and heat to boiling. Add the cornstarch mixture and cook, stirring continuously, until the sauce thickens, about 30 seconds. Dish out and serve immediately with steaming-hot rice.

JJ's Spicy-Crispy Tofu with Green Beans

My friend JJ is crazy for flavor, which makes sense because his personality is full of zest and zip! He loves the texture contrast between the crispy tofu and the tender green beans in this classic recipe so much I had to name it after him. Cubes of tofu are flash-fried and then tossed with green beans, garlic, ginger and onions in a delectably sweet, spicy and savory sauce.

Serves 4 as part of a multi-course meal
Preparation time: 10 minutes +
   blanching time
Cooking time: 15 minutes

8 oz (250 g) Chinese long beans or green
   beans, cut into 1-in (2.5-cm) pieces
2 tablespoons all-purpose flour
2 tablespoons all-purpose cornstarch
½ teaspoon salt
8 oz (250 g) firm tofu, drained, patted dry
   and cut into cubes
Oil for frying
1 clove garlic, minced
1 teaspoon peeled and minced fresh
   ginger
½ small white onion, cut into small chunks
½ teaspoon chili garlic sauce or sambal
   oelek
2 teaspoons soy sauce
2 teaspoons oyster sauce
1 teaspoon sugar
1 green onion (scallion), finely chopped

1 Blanch the beans in boiling water until tender-crisp (about 2 minutes for long beans, 5 minutes for green beans). Transfer with a slotted spoon to an ice water bath to cool, then drain and set aside.

2 Combine the flour, cornstarch and salt in a bowl. Toss the tofu pieces in the flour mixture. In a large wok or deep skillet, heat 2 to 3 inches (5 to 7.5 cm) of the oil to 350°F (175°C). Fry the tofu for 4 minutes, then turn it over and fry for another 4 minutes, or until golden brown all over. Drain on a sheet pan lined with paper towels. Set aside.

3 Remove all but 1 tablespoon of the oil from the wok or skillet, then heat over medium-high heat. Add the garlic, ginger and onion and stir-fry until fragrant and onion is translucent, about 1 minute. Add the fried tofu and stir-fry for 1 minute. Mix in the drained green beans, chili garlic sauce, soy sauce, oyster sauce and sugar and stir-fry for 1 more minute, then add the green onions and stir-fry for another 30 seconds. Dish out and serve immediately with steaming-hot rice.

Noodles and Rice

Noodles have been around in China since the Han Dynasty (206 BCE–220 CE), and their longstanding prominence in the cuisine makes it clear that the Chinese love their noodles! Luckily, Marco Polo brought noodles to the West after his historic voyage to China.

Slurped, twirled or sipped, noodles are enjoyed morning, noon and night in China. They symbolize longevity: Long-Life Noodles, served on birthdays and the Chinese New Year, are never cut (the longer the noodle, the longer the life). Some of my favorite childhood memories are of gobbling up steaming bowls of my mother's delicious Canton-Style Chicken Chow Mein (page 145) or Three-Flavor Lo Mein (page 136) on a cold day.

Rice is woven into the fabric of life for Chinese people. The grain is so revered that people greet each on the street by saying, "Have you eaten rice yet?" Rice is the core of virtually every Chinese meal and holds a place of honor at the table. Long-grain white rice is the standard in Chinese cuisine, but feel free to experiment with brown rice, jasmine rice or even quinoa.

I think plain, steaming-hot white rice accompanying my meat and vegetable dishes is sublime (see page 19 to learn how to make a perfect pot), but there is a rich tradition of other rice dishes in China, especially fried rice. My favorite fried-rice dishes include the juicy, bright and flavorful Pineapple Fried Rice (page 137) and the Farmers' Market Fried Brown Rice (page 147). And how could I forget the luxurious Crab Fried Rice (page 135) my mom used to make for us on special occasions?

Singapore Rice Noodles

I've been told that these noodles are a Cantonese creation; no one is quite sure how Singapore got involved in its name. This is an earthy dish made with rice noodles stir-fried with curry powder, bean sprouts, shrimp, BBQ pork and vegetables. Wherever these noodles came from, they are incredibly flavorful and easy to make. You can find them all over Hong Kong, in restaurants and open-air night-market stalls. When my mother first made these for me, the yellow color stood out immediately. She explained that it's one of the dish's unique characteristics, and it comes from the Madras curry powder. Try these noodles for your next dinner party and they're sure to be a standout.

Serves 4 to 6 as part of a multi-course meal
Preparation time: 15 minutes
Cooking time: 10 minutes

SAUCE
1 tablespoon Madras curry powder
2 tablespoons soy sauce
1 tablespoon Chinese rice wine or sherry
1 teaspoon sugar
4 tablespoons chicken stock, homemade (page 62) or store-bought
1 teaspoon dark sesame oil
2 teaspoons Asian chili sauce, such as Sriracha

10 oz (330 g) dried rice stick noodles
2 tablespoons oil, divided
2 large eggs, beaten
1 clove garlic, minced
2 teaspoons peeled and minced fresh ginger
1 small white onion, thinly sliced
8 shelled and deveined medium-sized raw shrimp
3½ oz (85 g) barbecued pork, homemade (page 41) or store-bought, thinly sliced
1 small red bell pepper, thinly sliced
1 cup (100 g) bean sprouts, ends trimmed
2 green onions (scallions), white and green parts, cut into 2-in (5-cm) pieces

1 Make the sauce: Combine all sauce ingredients in a small bowl and whisk until blended. Set aside.

2 Follow the directions for "Eliminating Shrimp's 'Fishy' Taste" on page 20. (This step is optional.)

3 Bring a large pot of water to a boil. Remove from the heat. Immerse the noodles in hot water and let stand, stirring occasionally, until they are soft, yet firm, about 10 minutes. Drain noodles well and rinse with water. Set aside.

4 Heat 1 tablespoon of the oil in a wok or skillet over medium-high heat. Pour in the eggs and swirl to coat the surface of the pan. Cook until set, 1 to 2 minutes. Cut the cooked egg into strips and halve the strips crosswise.

5 Heat the remaining oil in the wok or skillet over medium-high heat. Add the garlic, ginger and onion and stir-fry until fragrant, about 1 minute. Add the shrimp and stir-fry until it turns pink, about 3 minutes. Mix in the pork slices, bell pepper and bean sprouts and stir-fry for 1 minute. Add the sauce and the drained noodles and stir-fry for 30 seconds, and then stir in the cooked egg and green onions and stir-fry for 30 seconds more. Serve immediately.

Crab Fried Rice

After a week of soccer practice, laundry, homework, spelling tests, recipe testing, dishwashing and school fundraising on top of my day job, I sometimes just need a little luxury in my life (I'm sure most people can relate). A trip to the spa? —No time for that. Some champagne? —Maybe, but I'll fall asleep during lunch. My favorite way to treat myself is by whipping up my mother's simple and sophisticated Crab Fried Rice. It's an elegant and time-honored dish, bursting with fresh lump crab meat. I can imagine I'm an empress during the Qing Dynasty, enjoying every bite—until someone knocks their grape juice onto my feet.

Serves 4 to 6 as part of a multi-course meal
Preparation time: 10 minutes
Cooking time: 6 minutes

2 large eggs, slightly beaten
½ teaspoons salt
Dash of white pepper
2 tablespoons oil, divided
1 clove garlic, minced
1 teaspoon peeled and minced fresh ginger
3 cups (450 g) cooked and chilled white rice
2 tablespoons soy sauce
1 tablespoon oyster sauce
8 oz (250 g) fresh lump crabmeat, picked through for shell fragments
1 small red bell pepper, diced
½ cup (75 g) frozen peas, thawed
1 green onion (scallion), finely chopped
Salt, to taste
White pepper, to taste

COOK'S NOTE
To save time, include an extra order of rice when you get Chinese takeout, or make a double batch for dinner the night before, reserving half for later use. Microwave the rice just until warm and use it for making fried rice.

1 In a medium bowl, whisk together the eggs, salt and white pepper.

2 Heat 1 tablespoon of the oil in a wok or skillet over medium-high heat. Add the eggs. Cook, stirring, until the eggs have set but are still moist. Transfer to a plate and set aside.

3 Wash and thoroughly dry the wok or skillet, then heat the remaining 1 tablespoon oil over medium-high heat. Add the garlic and ginger and stir-fry until fragrant, about 30 seconds, then add the rice and stir-fry for 2 minutes. Pour in the soy sauce and oyster sauce and stir-fry for 30 seconds. Mix in the crabmeat, red bell pepper and peas and stir-fry for 1 minute, then add the cooked egg and green onion and stir-fry for 30 seconds more. Season to taste with salt and white pepper. Serve immediately.

Three-Flavor Lo Mein

Noodles symbolize longevity in Chinese culture, so noodles are always served on the Chinese New Year, as well as on birthdays. The longer the noodle, the longer the life, so noodles should be served uncut. Of course, my mother always served noodles at our birthday dinners, and I always begged her to make Three-Flavor Lo Mein for mine. Lo Mein literally translates as "tossed noodle." I love this recipe because it's tossed with my three favorite things: chicken, shrimp and barbecued pork, in a savory traditional Cantonese-style gravy.

Serves 6 as part of a multi-course meal
Preparation time: 20 minutes
Cooking time: 10 minutes

8 oz (250 g) dried egg noodles or 14 oz (400 g) fresh egg noodles (page 140)

3 tablespoons all-purpose cornstarch

3 tablespoons cold water

6 oz (150 g) snow peas, tips and strings removed

2 tablespoons oil

1 teaspoon peeled and minced fresh ginger

1 clove garlic, minced

4 stalks bok choy, trimmed cut diagonally into ½-in (1.25-cm) slices

4 oz (100 g) fresh shiitake mushrooms, stemmed and thinly sliced

4 tablespoons oyster sauce

1 teaspoon salt

1 cup (250 ml) chicken stock, homemade (page 62) or store-bought

8 shelled and deveined medium-sized cooked shrimp

4 oz (100 g) shredded cooked chicken breast

4 oz (100 g) sliced barbecued pork, homemade (page 41) or store-bought

2 green onions (scallions), green and white parts, cut into 1-in (5-cm) pieces

1 Preheat oven to 300°F (149°C).

2 Bring a large pot of water to a boil over high heat. Add the noodles and cook until almost al dente, about 5 minutes for dried noodles, 3 minutes for fresh. Drain well and set aside.

3 Transfer to a platter and place in oven to keep warm.

4 Mix the cornstarch and cold water together. Set aside.

5 Blanch the snow peas in boiling water until tender, about 1 minute. Using a slotted spoon, transfer to an ice water bath to cool, then drain and set aside.

6 Heat the oil in the wok or skillet over medium-high heat. Add the ginger and garlic and stir-fry until fragrant, about 30 seconds. Stir in the bok choy and mushrooms and stir-fry for 1 minute.

7 Add the oyster sauce, salt, chicken stock, shrimp, chicken and pork. Cook until the stock comes to a boil, then add the cornstarch mixture and continue to cook, stirring constantly, until the sauce thickens and all the ingredients are nicely coated. Add the blanched snow peas and green onions and stir-fry for 30 seconds more. Dish out over the noodles and serve immediately.

Pineapple Fried Rice

When my mom and I made this on the *Today* show a few years ago, it didn't occur to me to slice the underside of the pineapple before going on live television so it would be easier to cut on camera. Needless to say, it was a bit of a struggle to cut through that pineapple quickly, but Al Roker charmingly dubbed my huffing and puffing the "Everyday Chinese Cooking Workout"! I love this recipe because the presentation is so impressive—the rice is served right in the pineapple shell. The chunks of fresh pineapple are sweet, bright and refreshing, perfectly offsetting the saltiness of the soy sauce in this dish. Chicken, shrimp, mushrooms and egg round out this delicious and refreshing dish.

Serves 4 to 6 as part of a multi-course meal
Preparation time: 15 minutes
Cooking time: 10 minutes

1 whole pineapple
2 large eggs, slightly beaten
1 teaspoon salt, divided
Dash of white pepper
2 tablespoons oil, divided
3 cups (450 g) cooked and chilled white rice
2 tablespoons soy sauce
1 cup (150 g) cubed cooked shrimp
1 cup (150 g) cubed cooked chicken breast
6 white button mushrooms, sliced
½ cup (75 g) fresh or thawed frozen peas
2 green onions (scallions), finely chopped, plus more for garnish
Salt, to taste
White pepper, to taste

COOK'S NOTE
For best results, the rice should be chilled overnight before cooking this dish.

1 Cut the pineapple in half lengthwise. Following the rim, cut deeply around the inside of the pineapple, being careful not to pierce through the skin. Cut the flesh inside the pineapple into cubes by making long slices down the length of the pineapple and then make 1-inch- (2.5-cm-) wide crosscuts. Scoop out the flesh using a flat-edged spoon and reserve.

2 In a medium bowl, combine the eggs with ½ teaspoon of the salt and the pepper. Whisk to blend.

3 Heat 1 tablespoon of the oil in a wok or skillet over medium heat. Add the eggs and stir-fry until they have set, but are still moist. Transfer to a plate and set aside.

4 Wash and thoroughly dry the wok or skillet, then heat the remaining 1 tablespoon oil over medium-high heat. Add the cooked rice and stir-fry for 2 minutes. Mix in the soy sauce, shrimp, chicken, mushrooms, peas and the remaining ½ teaspoon salt and stir-fry for 2 to 3 minutes. Add the cooked eggs, reserved pineapple flesh and green onions and stir-fry for 30 seconds more. Season to taste with the salt and white pepper.

5 Scoop the fried rice into the pineapple halves and garnish with additional green onion. Serve immediately.

Dan Dan Noodles

This is a quintessential homestyle Sichuan dish, with ground meat stir-fried in a chili-laced sesame vinegar sauce. Dan Dan Noodles are sinfully delicious and traditionally very spicy. I had these for the first time when my parents brought us to a Sichuan restaurant in New York as kids. We had never tasted anything so spicy, and we started crying (shaming our parents for rearing children with bland, Midwestern palates). Fortunately, we all grew up to be Sriracha junkies. The amount of chili oil in this recipe is for someone who doesn't mind *some* heat, but feel free to adjust accordingly. The ground Sichuan Pepper adds a tingly heat to the noodles, and the Sichuan preserved vegetables add a slight bitter and sour edge to the dish. Both are optional, but they add surprising depth.

Serves 4 as a main course
Preparation time: 10 minutes
Cooking time: 10 minutes

8 oz (250 g) dried egg noodles or 12 oz (350 g) fresh egg noodles (page 140)

SAUCE
2 tablespoons water
4 tablespoons chicken stock, homemade (page 62) or store-bought
2 tablespoons soy sauce
2 teaspoons smooth peanut butter
2 teaspoons Chinese sesame paste or tahini
1 tablespoon Chinese black vinegar or good quality balsamic vinegar
1 to 2 tablespoons chili oil, homemade (page 25) or store-bought
2 teaspoons dark sesame oil
¼ teaspoon five-spice powder
1 teaspoon sugar
¼ teaspoon ground Sichuan pepper (optional)

2 teaspoons oil
1 clove garlic, minced
2 teaspoons peeled and minced fresh ginger
2 green onions (scallions), white and green parts separated, finely chopped
4 oz (100 g) ground pork or turkey
2 teaspoons Chinese rice wine or sherry
4 tablespoons crushed roasted peanuts
2 tablespoons canned Sichuan preserved vegetables, finely chopped (optional)

1 Bring a large pot of water to a boil over high heat. Add the noodles and cook until almost al dente, about 5 minutes for dried noodles, 3 minutes for fresh. Drain well and set aside.

2 Make the sauce: In a small saucepan, bring the water and chicken stock to a boil. Add the remaining sauce ingredients and combine until blended. Remove from heat.

3 Distribute the noodles evenly among four bowls. Pour the sauce over the noodles and toss to coat with the sauce. Set aside.

4 Heat the oil in a wok or skillet over medium high heat. Add the garlic, ginger and green onions (white parts) and stir-fry until fragrant, about 1 minute. Add the ground pork and stir-fry until the meat is no longer pink, about 4 minutes. Add the rice wine or sherry and stir-fry for 1 minute more, then remove from heat.

5 Spoon the cooked meat mixture over the noodles. Garnish with the green onions (green parts), peanuts and Sichuan preserved vegetables, if using, and serve immediately.

Kung Pao Tofu Noodles

My sister Laura gave me the idea for turning everybody's favorite Chinese dish, Kung Pao, into a noodle recipe. I was throwing a dinner party and I still needed a noodle dish, but my kids were begging for Kung Pao Chicken—*and* our vegetarian friends were coming by! Laura said, "Why don't you just make everyone happy and whip up some Kung Pao Noodles with Tofu?" The rest is noodle history. My vegetarian friends were thrilled because they had missed enjoying all the flavors in Kung Pao, but had never thought to make it with tofu. Now, I call that using your noodle!

Serves 4 as part of a multi-course meal
Preparation time: 10 minutes
Cooking time: 10 minutes

8 oz (250 g) dried egg noodles or 12 oz (350 g) fresh egg noodles (page 140)

SAUCE
4 tablespoons Chinese black vinegar
4 tablespoons tablespoon vegetable stock
2 teaspoons sugar
3 tablespoons Chinese rice wine or sherry
2 tablespoons hoisin sauce, homemade (page 25) or store-bought
1 tablespoon oyster sauce
1 tablespoons soy sauce
2 teaspoons dark sesame oil
2 teaspoons all-purpose cornstarch
2 teaspoons water

2 tablespoons oil, divided
One 16-oz (550-g) block firm tofu, drained, patted dry and cut into cubes
1 clove garlic, minced
½ teaspoon crushed red pepper
1 large red bell pepper, diced
2 finely chopped green onions (scallions), white and green parts, plus more for garnish
1 cup (150 g) roasted peanuts, plus more for garnish

1 Bring a large pot of water to a boil over high heat. Add the noodles and cook until almost al dente, about 5 minutes for dried noodles, 3 minutes for fresh. Drain well and set aside.

2 Make the sauce: Combine all sauce ingredients in a small bowl and whisk to blend. Set aside.

3 Heat 1 tablespoon of the oil in the wok or skillet over medium-high heat. Add the tofu pieces and fry until brown on one side, about 3 minutes. Turn them over and cook for about 3 more minutes. Remove from the pan and set aside.

4 Wash and thoroughly dry the wok or skillet, then heat the remaining 1 tablespoon oil over medium-high heat. Add the garlic and stir-fry until fragrant, about 30 seconds. Mix in the crushed red pepper and stir-fry for another 30 seconds. Add the red bell pepper and stir-fry 2 minutes. Add the reserved tofu and stir gently for 30 seconds.

5 Add the cooked noodles and sauce. Cook, stirring to coat, for about 1 minute. Add the green onions and peanuts and stir for 30 seconds more, then remove from heat. Garnish with more green onions and peanuts and serve immediately.

COOK'S NOTE
If Chinese black vinegar is not available, balsamic vinegar can be substituted.

Vegetable Lo Mein

My friend Karen, a working mom who doesn't have much time to cook, tried these noodles at my house. She was amazed at how tender-crisp the vegetables were and how fresh and delicious everything tasted. She didn't believe she could make it herself until I had her over for a cooking lesson, along with our friend Rebecca. Armed with spatulas and glasses of pinot grigio, they finished the recipe and said, "Wow, did we really just do that?" My mother always taught me that Chinese cooking is all about the prep, so if you have all of the ingredients cut, cleaned and ready to go, you too will master this dish in no time. Cheers to that!

Serves 4 as part of a multi-course meal
Preparation time: 20 minutes
Cooking time: 10 minutes

8 oz (250 g) dried egg noodles or 14 oz (400 g) fresh egg noodles (page 140)
2 oz (50 g) snow peas, tips and strings removed
2 oz (50 g) broccoli florets
3 tablespoons all-purpose cornstarch
3 tablespoons cold water
2 tablespoons oil
1 teaspoon peeled and minced fresh ginger
1 clove garlic, minced
2 oz (50 g) sliced carrots
2 oz (50 g) fresh shiitake mushrooms, stemmed and thinly sliced
2 oz (50 g) thinly sliced red bell pepper
2 oz (50 g) canned baby corn, drained, rinsed and sliced lengthwise
4 tablespoons oyster sauce
1 cup (250 ml) vegetable stock or chicken stock, homemade (page 62) or store-bought
1 teaspoon salt
2 green onions (scallions), green and white parts, cut into 1-in (2.5-cm) pieces

1 Preheat oven to 300°F (149°C).

2 Bring a large pot of water to a boil over high heat. Add the noodles and cook until almost al dente, about 5 minutes for dried noodles, 3 minutes for fresh. Drain well and set aside.

3 Blanch the snow peas and broccoli florets in boiling water until tender, about 1 minute. Using a slotted spoon, transfer to an ice water bath to cool, then drain and set aside.

4 Mix the cornstarch and the cold water together and set aside.

5 Heat the oil in the wok or skillet over medium-high heat. Add the ginger and garlic and stir-fry until fragrant, about 30 seconds. Mix in the carrots and mushrooms and stir-fry for 3 minutes. Add the red bell pepper and baby corn and stir-fry for 1 minute.

6 Pour in the oyster sauce, vegetable or chicken stock and the salt. Cook until the stock comes to a boil, then add the cornstarch mixture and stir until the sauce thickens and all the ingredients are nicely coated. Add the drained snow peas and broccoli and the green onions and stir-fry for 30 seconds. Dish out over the noodles and serve immediately.

COOK'S NOTE
To save time and minimize waste, you can buy pre-cut and washed vegetables at the grocery store salad bar.

Homemade Egg Noodles

Making noodles is a fun rainy-day project for the whole family. These egg noodles are extremely versatile and can be used in a variety of soups and stir-fries, as well as any noodle recipe. You can boil them in chicken stock to make soup, or pan-fry them in oil and garlic and drizzle soy sauce over them, or top them with any stir-fry combination. They'll be delicious and satisfying no matter how you choose to prepare them!

Makes about 1 lb (450 g)
Preparation time: 20 minutes

1¼ cups (125 g) all-purpose flour or semolina flour
2 large eggs

1 In a medium bowl, mix together the flour and eggs to make a dough. Knead the dough on a lightly floured surface until elastic. Add a bit of water if necessary. Form into a ball and let rest for 15 minutes.

2 With a rolling pin, roll the dough into an oval sheet, rolling the dough from the center outward, until very thin. Place the dough on a lightly floured cloth so that one-third of it is on the cloth and two-thirds of it hangs off the edge of the table or counter. Using gravity to help, carefully stretch the dough out further.

3 Lightly flour the sheet of dough and roll it into a tube about 3 inches (7.5 cm) in diameter. Flatten the tube and use a sharp knife to slice the dough crosswise into very thin noodles. Separate the noodles and form them into a nest.

COOK'S NOTE
You can freeze homemade noodles for up to 3 months, or keep them for up to 2 days in the refrigerator.

Shrimp with Garlic Noodles

Okay, I know you're looking at the ingredient list and wondering why a Chinese recipe would call for Parmesan cheese. My mom and I had lunch once at an Asian restaurant in Beverly Hills, famous for its garlic noodles. It inspired us to create our own fusion version of this dish that I think tastes even better. The Parmesan adds a richness and marries pleasantly (albeit surprisingly) with traditional Chinese ingredients like soy sauce and sesame oil. A touch of sugar adds sweetness, and the fresh lime juice adds a bright note to the complex flavorings this dish.

Serves 4 as part of a multi-course meal
Preparation time: 8 minutes + marinating time
Cooking time: 10 minutes

8 oz (250 g) shelled and deveined large raw shrimp
⅛ teaspoon salt
1 teaspoon all-purpose cornstarch
½ teaspoon dark sesame oil
6 oz (175 g) dried egg noodles, or 10 oz (330 g) fresh egg
   noodles (page 140)
2 tablespoons oil, divided
4 cloves garlic, minced, divided
1 tablespoon soy sauce
½ teaspoon sugar
1 tablespoon freshly squeezed lime juice
⅓ cup (35 g) grated Parmesan cheese

1 Follow the directions for "Eliminating Shrimp's 'Fishy' Taste" on page 20. (This step is optional.)

2 Toss the shrimp with the salt, cornstarch and sesame oil. Cover and refrigerate for 20 minutes.

3 Bring a large pot of water to a boil over high heat. Add the noodles and cook until almost al dente, about 5 minutes for dried noodles, 3 minutes for fresh. Drain well and set aside.

4 Heat 1 tablespoon of the oil in a wok or skillet over medium-high heat. Add half of the garlic and stir-fry until fragrant, about 30 seconds. Reduce the heat to medium and add the egg noodles. Stir-fry for about 1 minute, tossing with a fork to separate and cook evenly. Turn off the heat. Add the soy sauce, sugar, lime juice and Parmesan cheese and toss to combine. Transfer to a serving platter.

5 Wash and thoroughly dry the wok, then heat the remaining 1 tablespoon oil over medium-high heat. Add the remaining 2 teaspoons garlic and stir-fry until fragrant, about 30 seconds. Add the shrimp and stir-fry for about 2 minutes, or until they turn pink. Remove the shrimp from the pan and arrange over the noodles. Serve immediately.

Beef Chow Fun

Fun means "wide rice noodle" in Chinese. The difference between this noodle dish and, say, chow mein or lo mein is that Chow Fun is made with flat, wide rice noodles which are chewy and fresh and soak up the flavor of the surrounding sauce. This is one of my favorite noodle dishes. It reminds of me of family lunches at our favorite *yum cha* (a restaurant that serves dim sum and literally means "drink tea") joints in Minneapolis that we went to after we got out of Chinese school (we frequently played hooky, which is why neither I nor my siblings can speak Chinese). Beef Chow Fun is a staple on *yum cha* menus. Loaded with lean beef, sweet asparagus and tender snow peas, it's a hearty, healthy one-dish meal.

Serves 2 to 3 as a main dish
Preparation time: 10 minutes + soaking and marinating time
Cooking time: 7 minutes

10 oz (330 g) fresh flat rice noodles (for dry noodles, see the Cook's Note following the method)
1 teaspoon dark sesame oil
3 medium dried black mushrooms
8 oz (250 g) beef tenderloin, sirloin steak or flank steak, sliced diagonally across the grain in ¼-in (6-mm) slices
1 teaspoon plus 2 tablespoons all-purpose cornstarch, divided
1¼ teaspoons salt, divided
2 teaspoons sugar, divided
Dash of white pepper
2 oz (50 g) snow peas, tips and strings removed
8 oz (250 g) asparagus, ends trimmed and cut into 2-in (5-cm) pieces
¾ cup (185 ml) chicken stock, homemade (page 62) or store-bought, divided
2 tablespoons oyster sauce
3 tablespoons oil, divided
1 teaspoon peeled and minced fresh ginger
1 clove garlic, minced
2 green onions (scallions), green and white parts, cut into 2-in (5-cm) pieces and then sliced lengthwise into thin strips, for garnish

1 Toss the noodles with the sesame oil. Divide the noodles evenly among 2 or 3 bowls (depending on the number of diners) and set aside.

2 Soak the mushrooms in hot water until soft, about 20 minutes, and drain. Remove and discard the stems and cut the caps into ½-inch (1.25-cm) pieces.

3 In a bowl, toss the beef, 1 teaspoon of the cornstarch, 1 teaspoon of the salt, 1 teaspoon of the sugar and the pepper. Cover and refrigerate for 20 minutes.

4 Bring a small saucepan of water to a boil. Add the snow peas and blanch for 1 minute or until tender-crisp. Using a slotted spoon, transfer the snow peas to a bowl of ice water and let cool completely. Drain and set aside.

5 In a small bowl, mix 4 tablespoons of the chicken stock with the remaining 2 tablespoons cornstarch, the remaining ¼ teaspoon salt, the oyster sauce and the remaining 1 teaspoon sugar. Set aside.

6 Heat 2 tablespoons of the oil in a wok or skillet over medium-high heat. Add the beef, ginger and garlic and stir-fry for 2 minutes. Remove the beef from the wok or skillet.

7 Wash and thoroughly dry the wok or skillet, then heat the remaining 1 tablespoon oil over medium-high heat. Add the drained mushrooms and the asparagus and stir-fry for 2 minutes. Pour in the remaining ½ cup (125 ml) chicken stock and the cornstarch mixture and cook, stirring continuously, until the sauce thickens and all ingredients are nicely coated, about 2 minutes.

8 Add the blanched snow peas and cook for 30 seconds. Add the beef and cook, stirring continuously, until the beef is hot. Pour the beef mixture evenly over the noodles in each bowl, garnish with the green onion strips and serve.

COOK'S NOTE
Substitute 6 oz (150 g) dried flat rice noodles for fresh noodles if you prefer. To prepare them, bring a large pot of water to a boil, then remove it from heat. Immerse the noodles in the hot water; let stand, stirring occasionally, until noodles are soft yet firm, about 10 minutes. Drain well and rinse with cool water.

Black Mushrooms and Broccoli with Egg Noodles

I try to get my kids to try new flavors all the time without making a big deal out of it. Sometimes this works; other times it doesn't. I remember wanting them to try black mushrooms to develop an appreciation for the savory taste, umami. When I showed them the hydrated black mushrooms, they said "Yuck," but then I remembered how my mom got us to try new things. I had them make the egg noodles from scratch with me for this dish. They were having so much fun rolling out and cutting the noodles they forgot all about their "yuck" comment. By the time I tossed the fresh noodles with the broccoli, black mushrooms and delicious oyster sauce-spiked gravy, they couldn't wait to dig in and gobble up their newest creation.

Serves 4 as part of a multi-course meal
Preparation time: 8 minutes + soaking time
Cooking time: 9 to 12 minutes

6 dried black mushrooms
¼ teaspoon salt
Dash of white pepper
½ teaspoon plus 2 tablespoons all-purpose cornstarch, divided
10 oz (330 g) broccoli florets
2 tablespoons oyster sauce
2 tablespoons water
2 tablespoons oil, divided
8 oz (250 g) dried egg noodles or 14 oz (400 g) fresh egg noodles (page 140)
2 cloves garlic, minced
2 tablespoons dry white wine
1 cup (250 ml) chicken stock, homemade (page 62) or store-bought
1 green onion (scallion), trimmed and cut into thin strips, for garnish

1 Soak the dried mushrooms in hot water for 20 minutes, or until soft. Discard the stems and cut the caps into thin strips. In a medium bowl, combine the mushrooms with the salt, pepper and ½ teaspoon of the cornstarch.

2 Bring a small saucepan of water to a boil. Add the broccoli and blanch for 1 minute, or until tender-crisp. Using a slotted spoon, transfer to a bowl of ice water to cool, then drain and set aside.

3 In a small bowl, mix together the remaining 2 tablespoons cornstarch, the oyster sauce and 2 tablespoons water.

4 Bring a large pot of water to a boil over high heat. Add the noodles and cook until almost al dente, about 5 minutes for dried noodles, 3 minutes for fresh. Drain well and set aside.

5 Heat 1 tablespoon of the oil in a wok or skillet over medium-high heat. Add the noodles and cook until the underside is browned, about 3 minutes. Flip over and brown the other side, 2 to 3 minutes more. Transfer to a platter.

6 Heat the remaining oil in the wok or skillet. Add the garlic and mushrooms and stir-fry for 1 minute. Add the white wine and stir-fry for another 30 seconds. Stir in the broccoli and chicken stock and bring to a boil.

7 Stir in the cornstarch mixture and cook, stirring constantly until the sauce thickens and all the ingredients are nicely coated, about 1 minute. Pour the mushrooms and sauce over the noodles, garnish with the green onions and serve immediately.

COOK'S NOTE
You can use leftover chicken, barbecued pork or seafood to this recipe. Just cut the meat into small pieces and add it before the chicken broth to make a complete meal in one dish.

Sesame Noodles with Chicken

Who doesn't love noodles, especially when they're tossed with peanut butter, sesame oil, soy sauce, garlic, ginger and some chili garlic sauce? This recipe is sweet and nutty with a nice spicy kick. It's super easy for a weeknight—all you need to do is toss in some shredded rotisserie chicken with whatever veggies you may have on hand. I like the texture of crunchy peanut butter, but feel free to use smooth peanut butter if that's what you prefer.

Serves 4 as part of a multi-course meal or for lunch
Preparation time: 25 minutes
Cooking time: 8 to 13 minutes

8 oz (250 g) dried Chinese egg noodles or spaghetti
5 oz (150 g) broccoli florets
½ cup (125 g) crunchy peanut butter
¾ cup (185 ml) chicken stock, homemade (page 62) or store-bought
1 teaspoon dark sesame oil
2 tablespoons soy sauce
2 cloves garlic, minced
1 tablespoon chili garlic sauce
2 teaspoons peeled and minced fresh ginger
5 oz (150 g) red bell pepper, thinly sliced
5 oz (150 g) carrots, cut into matchsticks
2 cups (300 g) shredded rotisserie chicken

1 Cook the noodles according to package directions. Drain well and rinse with cool water.

2 Blanch the broccoli florets in boiling water until tender, about 1 minute. Using a slotted spoon, transfer the broccoli to an ice water bath to cool, then drain and set aside.

3 Whisk the peanut butter, chicken stock, sesame oil, soy sauce, garlic, chili garlic sauce and ginger together in a large bowl.

4 Add the noodles, vegetables and shredded chicken to the sauce and toss to combine all ingredients. Serve warm or chilled.

COOK'S NOTE
You can save time by purchasing prewashed, precut veggies from the salad bar at your local grocery store.

Canton-Style Chicken Chow Mein

To me, this is the ultimate Chinese comfort food. When we were young, my mom worked sixty to seventy hours a week, earning fifty cents an hour as a seamstress, so she had hardly any leisure time. On those rare Saturdays when she had some time off, she'd make big steaming bowls of her delicious chow mein for lunch. This dish showcases Cantonese noodles at their best. The egg noodles are pan-fried on both sides so they're crispy on the outside, but still soft and tender on the inside. The noodles are then topped with stir-fried chicken, garlic, ginger, bean sprouts, shiitake mushrooms and snow peas in a smooth and savory gravy. Okay, just writing this is making me ravenous and I'm off (to make some chow mein)!

Serves 4 as part of a multi-course meal
Preparation time: 20 minutes
Cooking time: 10 minutes

8 oz (250 g) boneless, skinless chicken breast or thigh, cut into thin strips
¼ teaspoon salt
⅛ teaspoon white pepper
1 teaspoon peeled and minced fresh ginger
1 teaspoon plus 2 tablespoons all-purpose cornstarch, divided
4 oz (100 g) snow peas, tips and strings removed
2 tablespoons oyster sauce
¼ teaspoon sugar
6 oz (175 g) dried egg noodles or 10 oz (330 g) fresh egg noodles (page 140)
4 tablespoons oil, divided
1 clove garlic, minced
2 oz (50 g) fresh shiitake mushrooms, stemmed and thinly sliced
6 oz (150 g) bean sprouts, ends trimmed
1 cup (250 ml) chicken stock, homemade (page 62) or store-bought

1 Toss the chicken with the salt, pepper, ginger and 1 teaspoon of the cornstarch. Cover and refrigerate for 20 minutes.

2 Blanch the snow peas in boiling water until tender, about 1 minute. Using a slotted spoon, transfer to an ice water bath to cool, then drain and set aside.

3 In a small bowl, combine the oyster sauce with the remaining 2 tablespoons cornstarch and the sugar.

4 Bring a large pot of water to a boil over high heat. Add the noodles and cook until almost al dente, about 5 minutes for dried noodles, 3 minutes for fresh. Drain well and set aside.

5 Heat 2 tablespoons of the oil in a wok or skillet over medium-high heat. Add the noodles and separate to cover the bottom of the pan, forming a large pancake. Fry until brown, about 3 minutes, and turn over. Brown the other side for 3 minutes, then transfer to a platter.

6 Heat the remaining 2 tablespoons oil in the wok or skillet over medium-high heat. Add the chicken and garlic and stir-fry for 1 minute. Stir in the mushrooms and bean sprouts and stir-fry for 2 minutes.

7 Pour in the chicken stock and heat until boiling. Add the cornstarch mixture and cook, stirring constantly, until the sauce thickens and all the ingredients are nicely coated. Add the drained snow peas and stir-fry for 30 seconds more. Dish out and serve immediately.

Quinoa Fried Rice

This dish doesn't have any rice in it, but I call it Quinoa Fried Rice because it uses a traditional Chinese fried-rice technique to prepare the quinoa. When my friend Carol was trying to get her kids, Kaj and Sebastian, to eat more protein, I told her to try this recipe. Her kids love fried rice, and this recipe tastes just like it, but it's loaded with healthy protein. Quinoa on its own is a bit nutty but rather bland. However, it soaks up all of the seasonings around it, and this dish is chock-full of flavor, as well as all sorts of other yummy stuff like ham, mushrooms and peas. The fish sauce lends a Southeast Asian note, making it a nice way to step out of the ordinary on a busy weeknight. This recipe is great for leftovers—dice up a cup of last night's roast chicken, grilled steak or leftover seafood and toss it in!

Serves 4 as part of a multi-course meal
Preparation time: 10 minutes
Cooking time: 7 minutes

2 large eggs, slightly beaten
½ teaspoon salt
Dash of white pepper
2 tablespoons oil, divided
1 clove garlic, minced
1 teaspoon peeled and minced fresh ginger
3 cups (550 g) cooked and chilled quinoa
1 tablespoon soy sauce
1 tablespoon fish sauce
1 cup (150 g) diced ham
½ cup (75 g) fresh or thawed frozen peas
6 white button mushrooms, sliced
2 green onions (scallions), finely chopped, plus more for garnish
Salt, to taste
White pepper, to taste

COOK'S NOTE
To prepare the quinoa, simply stir 1 cup of rinsed, uncooked quinoa into 2 cups of boiling water, cover and simmer over low heat until done. This will yield 3 cups of cooked quinoa.

1 In a medium bowl, combine the eggs with the salt and pepper.

2 Heat 1 tablespoon of the oil a wok or skillet over medium heat. Add the eggs and stir-fry until they are set but still moist. Transfer to a plate and set aside.

3 Wash and thoroughly dry the wok or skillet, then heat the remaining 1 tablespoon oil over medium-high heat. Add the garlic and ginger and stir-fry until fragrant, about 30 seconds. Add the quinoa and stir-fry for 2 minutes. Mix in the soy sauce, fish sauce, ham, peas and mushrooms and stir-fry for 2 minutes. Add the reserved eggs and green onions and stir-fry for 30 seconds. Season to taste with salt and white pepper. Dish out, garnish with additional green onions and serve immediately.

Farmers' Market Fried Brown Rice

My mother was an early proponent of the farm-to-fork (whoops, I mean chopstick) philosophy. Raised by eating off the land—i.e., her family's vegetable garden—she always believed that the freshest food is the best food. With the proliferation of farmer's markets and CSAs, it's easier than ever to support local agriculture and buy the freshest produce possible. Farmers' Market Fried Brown Rice celebrates the variety of vegetables available at farmers' markets. The colors and textures from the array of vegetables in this dish make for a beautiful presentation. Feel free to experiment with your favorite veggies from your local farmers' market. Let's eat the rainbow!

Serves 4 to 6 as part of a multi-course meal
Preparation time: 25 minutes
Cooking time: 10 minutes

3 large egg whites
½ teaspoon salt
Dash of white pepper
3 tablespoons oil, divided
1 small shallot, minced
1 teaspoon peeled and minced fresh ginger
4 oz (100 g) carrots, sliced thinly on a diagonal
1 small red bell pepper, diced
4 oz (100 g) asparagus spears, trimmed and finely chopped
4 oz (100 g) thinly sliced white button mushrooms
4 oz (100 g) sugar snap peas
3 cups (450 g) cooked and chilled brown rice
1 teaspoon dark sesame oil
4 teaspoons soy sauce
1 tablespoon unseasoned rice vinegar or white vinegar
4 tablespoons green onions (scallions), finely chopped (white and green parts)
Salt, to taste
White pepper, to taste

1 In a small bowl, combine the egg whites with the salt and white pepper. Whisk to blend.

2 Heat 1 tablespoon of the oil in a wok or skillet over medium-high heat. Add the egg whites. Stir-fry until the egg whites are set but still moist. Transfer to a plate and set aside.

3 Blanch the sugar snap peas in boiling water until tender, about 1 minute. Using a slotted spoon, transfer to an ice water bath to cool, then drain and set aside.

4 Wash and thoroughly dry the wok or skillet, then heat the remaining 2 tablespoons oil over medium-high heat. Add the shallots and ginger and stir-fry until fragrant, about 30 seconds.

Add the carrots and stir-fry for 1 minute, then stir in the red bell pepper, asparagus and mushrooms and stir-fry for 2 minutes. Add the sugar snap peas and stir-fry for 30 seconds.

5 Mix in the rice and stir-fry for 2 minutes, then pour in the sesame oil, soy sauce, rice vinegar and green onions and stir-fry for 30 seconds more. Season to taste with salt and white pepper. Serve immediately.

Drinks and Desserts

Growing up in America, we rebelled against the traditional Chinese desserts our parents tried to serve us, like red bean soup or almond tofu pudding. These flavors and textures just didn't appeal to our Americanized palates. In my mother's China, there was no ice cream, strawberry short cake, chocolate chip cookies or banana cream pies. Frustrated, she'd put down a plate of sliced oranges—another traditional way to end a Chinese meal—shrug her shoulders and walk away. We were the product of 1970s America, and we wanted Jell-O parfaits!

Over time, my mother adapted and created Asian fusion desserts for her catering clients, and we became her willing guinea pigs. We'd help her dip fortune cookies in chocolate and stuff them with personalized fortunes—often in Hebrew—for her Bar and Bat Mitzvah gigs. When she and I started our catering business together, we collaborated on new dessert creations. I'm excited to share recipes like Chilled Berry Tea (page 150), a light, refreshing berry concoction laced with passion fruit tea and star anise, and Banana-Walnut Wontons (page 153)—my twins, Becca and Dylan's favorite, especially when they're served over French vanilla ice cream. Finally, I'm thrilled to share the recipe for Five-Spice Chocolate Cake (page 155) from my friend Theresa, a pastry chef. It's rich, exotic and absolutely scrumptious.

Chilled Berry Tea

The combination of star anise, berries, bananas and passion fruit tea in this dessert is intoxicatingly delicious and hard to describe. It has an elixir-like quality, and is incredibly refreshing after a big meal. My mother and I once made this for 300 people at an outdoor symphony benefit. Even though we felt like we were cooking in the woods, it was totally worth it when we kept hearing, "Wow, that tea!" "Extraordinary!" and "That was incredible!" after it was served. Try this and I promise it will be music to your ears—I mean, your taste buds!

Makes 6 servings
Preparation time: 5 minutes
Cooking time: 5 minutes

1½ cups (375 ml) water
5 star anise pods
1¼ cups (280 g) sugar
2 bags passion fruit tea
3 cups (300 g) mixed berries
    (strawberries, blueberries, raspberries,
    blackberries)
½ cup (75 g) diced bananas
Fresh mint leaves, for garnish

1 Combine the water and the star anise in a medium saucepan and bring to a boil over high heat. Cook for 2 minutes, then add the sugar and stir well until the sugar is dissolved. Return to a full boil, then turn off the heat and place the tea bags in the syrup. Stir, cover and allow to cool. Remove the tea bags and the star anise.

2 Distribute the berries and bananas evenly among 6 martini glasses. Pour the cooled tea over the berries and bananas and refrigerate until ready to serve. Garnish with mint leaves before serving.

Banana Spring Rolls with Chocolate-Ginger Sauce

This crisp, light and sweet dessert is easy to make and always goes over well at dinner parties. I love the zing of ginger in the chocolate sauce. My mom taught me how to cut the spring roll wrappers into fourths to make miniature cigar-shaped banana spring rolls, which are great for the little ones because they fit neatly in their hands. Unfortunately for me (and fortunately for them), my six year-old twins were the guinea pigs, and they drove me bananas with requests for more!

Serves 4
Preparation time: 10 minutes
Cooking time: 22 minutes

CHOCOLATE-GINGER SAUCE

1 cup (250 ml) heavy cream
3 tablespoons brown sugar
4 tablespoons peeled and minced fresh
   ginger
6 oz (175 g) semisweet chocolate chips or
   semisweet chocolate, chopped or grated

4 spring roll wrappers
4 ripe bananas, sliced crosswise into thirds
2 teaspoons freshly squeezed lemon juice
Water
Oil for frying
Powdered sugar for dusting
Fresh mint leaves for garnish

1 Make the sauce: Bring the heavy cream, brown sugar and ginger to a gentle boil in a small saucepan over medium heat, stirring to dissolve the brown sugar. Reduce the heat to medium-low and simmer, covered, for 15 minutes, stirring occasionally.

2 Strain the mixture through a fine-mesh sieve, then return it to the saucepan and stir in the chocolate. Bring to a simmer over medium-low heat, stirring continuously, until the chocolate melts. Remove from the heat.

3 Sprinkle the banana pieces with lemon juice to prevent browning. Separate the spring roll wrappers and place them under a damp towel. Lay one spring roll wrapper out on a clean work surface. Place 3 banana pieces in a straight line across the bottom third of the wrapper. Start rolling the wrapper tightly, folding in the edges as you go along, to form a uniform cylinder. Seal the last tip with a little water. Repeat with the remaining bananas. Place in a covered container in the refrigerator until ready to cook.

4 In a wok or deep skillet, heat 2 to 3 inches (5 to 7.5 cm) oil to 350°F (175°C). Deep-fry the spring rolls until golden brown, from 1 to 2 minutes, turning frequently. Place on a wire rack to cool. Warm the sauce over medium-low heat, if necessary. Cut each spring roll in half at an angle, arrange on a plate and dust with powdered sugar. Drizzle with the warm chocolate-ginger sauce and garnish with mint leaves. Serve immediately.

Chocolate-Raspberry Wontons

Ah, Nutella. How do I love thee? Let me count the ways.... Number one, you make a fantastic filling for Chocolate-Raspberry Wontons. Raspberries and chocolate-hazelnut spread go together like Sonny and Cher, and they make beautiful music together in this luscious dessert. When my friend Christos threw a launch party for his new clothing line, we served Chocolate-Raspberry Wontons, and his fans went wild. Every bite of these creamy, chocolaty wonton pillows is insanely delicious; when topped with the raspberry sauce, they're out of this world.

Serves 8
Preparation time: 25 minutes
Cooking time: 8 to 10 minutes

RASPBERRY SAUCE
4 cups (500 g) fresh raspberries
½ cup (125 ml) water
¾ cup (185 ml) sugar
2 tablespoons all-purpose cornstarch

⅓ cup (40 g) chopped fresh raspberries
⅔ cup (200 g) chocolate-hazelnut spread such as Nutella
16 round dumpling wrappers
1 egg, lightly beaten
Oil for frying
Confectioner's sugar for garnish
Mint leaves for garnish

1 Make the sauce: Place the 4 cups (500 g) raspberries in a small saucepan. Crush the berries and add the water. Stir in the sugar and cornstarch and bring to a boil over medium heat, stirring constantly. Remove from heat and press through a strainer. Set the sauce aside.

2 Fold the ⅓ cup chopped raspberries into the chocolate-hazelnut spread until combined. Lay a dumpling wrapper on a clean work surface and brush the edges with egg. Place 1 scant tablespoon of chocolate-hazelnut raspberry mixture in the center, then fold the wrapper in half over and the filling, pressing the edges firmly to seal. Repeat with remaining wrappers and filling.

3 In a wok or deep skillet heat 2 to 3 inches (5 to 7.5 cm) of the oil to 350°F (175°C). Deep-fry the wontons until golden brown, 1 to 2 minutes, turning occasionally. Place on a paper-towel-lined sheet pan to drain. Transfer to a platter and dust with confectioner's sugar, then drizzle with raspberry sauce. Garnish with mint leaves and serve immediately.

COOK'S NOTE
If you only can find square wonton wrappers, use a cookie cutter to cut them into rounds.

Banana-Walnut Wontons

A client asked us to make an Asian-inspired dessert as a birthday surprise for his wife, using her favorite ingredients; bananas and walnuts. We scratched our heads for a while until my mother said, "I know! Let's make Banana-Walnut Wontons." Using store-bought candied walnuts makes this dessert super easy, even though it's divinely decadent. We served the wontons in individual martini glasses that night over French vanilla ice cream drizzled with chocolate sauce.

Makes 6 to 8 servings
Preparation time: 10 minutes
Cooking time: 2 minutes

2 ripe bananas, diced
2 tablespoons sugar
4 tablespoons candied or glazed walnuts, roughly
   chopped
1 large egg, slightly beaten
20 wonton wrappers
Oil for frying
2 tablespoons cinnamon sugar, for topping
Store-bought chocolate sauce, for topping

1 Toss the bananas with the sugar and the candied walnuts.

2 Lay a wonton wrapper on a clean work surface and brush the edges with beaten egg. Place 2 teaspoons of the banana mixture in the center of the wrapper. Pull the four corners together and pinch firmly to make a pouch, making sure all the edges are sealed. Repeat with all the wonton wrappers and filling.

3 In a wok or deep skillet, heat 2 to 3 inches (5 to 7.5 cm) of the oil to 350°F (175°C). Fry 6 wontons at a time until golden brown, about 2 or 3 minutes. Remove from the oil and transfer to a paper-towel-lined sheet pan. Repeat with the remaining wontons. Sprinkle with cinnamon sugar and drizzle with chocolate sauce before serving.

Lychee and Ginger Sorbet

My mother used to tell me about eating lychee nuts with her friends on hot summer days when she was growing up in China. I'll always have a fondness for lychees because they make me think of Mom being young and carefree. Although this dessert is easy, it takes a little time. Trust me, though: it's worth it. It's a refined and refreshing finish to a heavy Chinese meal, and your guests will "Ooh" and "Ahhh" at your magical sorbet-making talents.

Serves 6
Preparation time: 10 minutes +
*   refrigerating and freezing time*

One 20-oz (560-g) can lychees
1 tablespoon freshly squeezed lime juice
1 teaspoon finely grated fresh ginger
Fresh mint leaves for garnish

1 Combine the lychees and their syrup with the lime juice and ginger in a food processor and process until smooth.

Transfer to a bowl and refrigerate for 2 hours to chill and allow the flavors to mingle.

2 Place in the freezer for 2 hours. Loosen up the mixture with a fork and return to the freezer. Freeze until solid, at least 4 more hours and up to overnight.

3 Remove from the freezer 10 minutes before serving to allow the mixture to soften. Scoop into glasses and garnish with mint leaves. Serve immediately.

Asian Pear Tart

My grandmother used to watch Chinese soap operas while savoring a dish of sliced Asian pears in our living room. Asian pears have a mild flavor that's similar to jicama, but sweeter, and a delicate crunch and a firmer texture than most pears. This tart is the perfect end to a Chinese meal. Just when you think it can't be topped, the ginger-spiked whipped cream does just that.

Serves 4
Preparation time: 30 minutes + chilling time
Cooking time: 30 minutes

GINGER CREAM
4 tablespoons water
3 tablespoons peeled and minced fresh ginger
1½ tablespoons sugar
1 cup (250 ml) chilled whipping cream

PEAR TART
3 ripe but firm Asian pears, peeled, cored and thinly sliced
2 teaspoons flour
2 tablespoons sugar
¼ teaspoon ground ginger
⅛ teaspoon salt
One 17.3-oz (490 g) package frozen puff pastry, thawed
3 tablespoons melted butter

1 Make the Ginger Cream: Combine the water, ginger and sugar in a small saucepan over medium heat. Stir until sugar dissolves, then simmer until mixture becomes syrupy, about 5 minutes. Cool completely.

2 Using an electric mixer, beat the whipping cream in a medium bowl until peaks form, then fold in the ginger syrup. Cover and chill in the refrigerator for at least 30 minutes and up to four hours.

3 Make the Pear Tart: Preheat oven to 375°F (190°C). Toss the pear slices with the flour, sugar, ginger and salt in a medium bowl.

4 Line four 4-inch (10-cm) tart dishes with the puff pastry. Lightly prick the surface with a fork. Lay the pear slices in decorative, overlapping circles on top of the crust, leaving a 1-inch (2.5-cm) border around the edge. Brush the pears with the melted butter. Bake for 30 minutes, or until pastry is golden brown. Serve warm or at room temperature with the ginger cream.

Stir the ginger cream ingredients (except the cream) over medium heat.

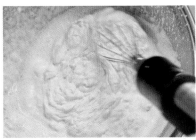

Beat the cream in a medium bowl until peaks form. Fold in the ginger mixture.

Toss the pear slices with the flour, sugar, ginger and salt.

Lay slices in a circle atop puff pastry. Brush with melted butter and bake.

Five-Spice Chocolate Cake

My pastry chef friend Theresa does it again! She contributed the fantastic Coconut Cake with Mango Sauce recipe to my last cookbook (*Everyday Thai Cooking*—Tuttle), and now she brings us this exotic Five-Spice Chocolate Cake. Moist, rich and sultry, this cake is to die for. Top with ginger cream (see opposite page) or some French vanilla ice cream, and you'll be in heaven.

Serves 6 to 8
Preparation time: 15 minutes
Cooking time: 40 to 45 minutes

2 cups (250 g) all-purpose flour
1 teaspoon baking powder
1 teaspoon baking soda
½ teaspoon salt
4 teaspoons five-spice powder
6 oz (175 g) bittersweet chocolate, chopped
½ cup (125 ml) strongly brewed hot coffee
1 cup (250 ml) buttermilk, at room temperature
1 teaspoon vanilla extract
2 large eggs, at room temperature
2 cups (400 g) sugar, plus extra for dusting pan
½ cup (60 g) semi-sweet chocolate chips
Powdered sugar for dusting

1 Preheat oven to 350°F (190°C). Butter and sugar a 10-inch (25-cm) round cake pan. Set aside.

2 In a large bowl, whisk together the flour, baking powder, baking soda, salt and five-spice powder. Set aside.

3 Place the chopped chocolate in a small bowl and pour the hot coffee over. Stir until the chocolate has melted. Add the buttermilk and vanilla and whisk to blend. Set aside.

4 In the bowl of a stand-up mixer, beat the eggs and sugar until light in color, about 3 minutes on medium-high speed. Add the chocolate-buttermilk mixture and mix to combine.

5 Add the flour mixture and mix on low until fully incorporated, scraping the sides of the bowl as necessary. Fold in the chocolate chips.

6 Pour the batter into the prepared cake pan. Place in oven on the middle rack and bake for 40 to 45 minutes. Allow to cool completely before turning out of the pan. Dust with powdered sugar before serving.

Index

Resource Guide

Luckily, you can find most of the staple ingredients you need for Chinese cooking at your neighborhood grocery store, with only an occasional trip to your local Asian market needed. If you don't live near an Asian market or for sheer convenience, there are many online resources available these days. Need some Sichuan Peppercorns in a hurry? Bam! You can get them delivered to your doorstep in two days from Amazon.com. I've included resources for ingredients, cooking tools and specialty products as well. Some of these on-line resources offer Asian and Chinese-inspired dishware and tableware to enhance your Chinese dining experience. I've also listed some of my favorite Chinese cookbooks that I cherish and have provided much knowledge, inspiration and creativity throughout my Chinese culinary journey.

Chinese Ingredients, Utensils and Tools

Import Food
www.importfood.com

Asian Food Grocer
www.asianfoodgrocer.com

Asian Supermarket 365
www.asiansupermarket365.com

Asian Wok
www.asianwok.com

The Wok Shop
www.wokshop.com/store

Wok Star
www.wokstar.us

World Market
www.worldmarket.com

Chinese Cookbooks

Mastering the Art of Chinese Cooking by Eileen Yin-Fei Lo

The Breath of a Wok by Grace Young

Easy Chinese Recipes by Bee Yinn Low

Chinese Cooking by Ken Hom

The Key to Chinese Cooking by Irene Kuo

My late mother Leeann and I on the set of our PBS cooking series, *Double Happiness.*

Acknowledgments

"Tell me and I'll forget, show me and I may remember, involve me and I'll understand." —Chinese proverb

I have so many people to thank for this book but I am most grateful to my late mother Leeann. As if she was answering to a higher calling (the Kitchen God, perhaps?), she made it her steadfast mission in life to instill a love of Chinese cooking in her children. She could have done this purely by example, we as the willing and appreciative participants watching with amazement at her culinary prowess in the kitchen. This would not be the case. I can remember being five years old standing by her side while she showed me how to fold creases in her delicious potstickers. She'd watch patiently and work with me until I felt comfortable, practicing over and over again. In these early moments together, I began to understand.

This book would never have happened without the love and support of my husband Matthew. He loved my mother as much as he loved her cooking and despite the craziness of our lives, he encouraged me to write this book as a means of healing and because he knows how huge a gift my mother's recipes are to the world.

I could have never completed this book without the passion and dedication of my posse of recipe testers. They never complained and always gave me swift and honest feedback: Stacy Mears, Jeanie Chin, Jack Fike, Billy Chin, Laura Chin, Jodi Young, Eleni Jankosky, and Theresa Frederickon.

To my siblings who helped test this book, I love you. I know that because we're Chinese we're not supposed to say this to

My mom signing one of her cookbooks.

My mom and I teaching a dim sum class at my house in Los Angeles.

On the set of one of my *Chef Katie Chin* Youtube shoots.

My elegant mom at one of her buffet restaurants.

one another, but I did anyway. So there! Special props to my former sous chef Stacy who moved last year to Austin, TX. Despite the geographical distance, her encouragement via Skype and email helped me overcome any obstacles that stood in my way.

I am indebted to Michele Speigel who worked tirelessly to edit and organize this book and make sense of my jumbled notes.

To Raghavan Iyer, thank you for your touching Foreword, and also for talking me off the ledge in the final stretch of writing this book. Having known my mother, you knew how emotional this process was for me and got me through it with warmth and humor.

Many people ask me how I get it all done. I'm no different than any other working mom, but I'd never survive without my A team. By "A team," I mean our kick-ass housekeeper, Delfina Garcia, who spent hours cleaning up after my testing sessions and keeping our lives in order. I'd also like to thank our au pair, Claudia Solano Vargas, who cared for our kids—especially as I burned the midnight

oil. To all the Hesby moms and dads: Thanks for all the carpooling, play dates and sleepovers!

I'd like to thank my children: Kyla, Dylan and Becca. Your love and support mean the world to me and I appreciate your patience after eating twenty stir-fries in a row.

Many thanks to all of my dear friends who lift me up and support me no matter what: Sophie Ali, Kimberly Barth, Nicole Behne, Pamela Brown, Alex Chen, Logan Chin, Traci Ching, Diana Choi, Michael Dagnery, Wendy Diamond, Joan Donatelle, Rita Drucker, Marissa Durazzo, Greg Economos, Leslie Fram, Christos Garkinos, Christopher Gordon, Paul Hemstreet, Devery Holmes, Sabrina Ironside, Brad Jamison, Eleni Jankowsky, Scott Joyce, Laura Keller, Erika Penzer Kerekes, Fumi Kitahara, Stacie Krajchir, George Leon, Rob Levine, Heather Reid Liebo, Frank Lomento, Jeannie Mai, Dave Marchi, Patrick Martin, Carol Cheng Mayer, JJ McKay, Carla Moreira, Carol Morejon, Neil Newman, Kristin Nicholas, Jen Nolander, Michael Now, Harry Parrish, Steve Patscheck, Peter Petraglia, Hugo

Rojas, Susie Romano, Rich Ross, Mary Sadeghy, Susan Safier, Adam Sanderson, Elayne Sawaya, Robert Schuller, Nicole Hirsty Seine, Valerie Shavers, Dennis Shortt, Mimi Slavin, Pam Slay, Terry Stanley, Andrea Stein, Michael Stone, Cynthia Sutter, Marianne Szymanski, Laura Takaragawa, Rosemary Tarquinio, Bil Tocantins, Trish Vogel, Mary Wagstaff, Katie Workman and Greg Yale.

Finally, I'd like to thank the team at Tuttle Publishing who made this dream become a reality in such a gorgeous and meaningful way. Thank you to my editors, Jon Steever and Katherine Heins, and also Christopher Johns, June Chong, Irene Ho, Anna Perotti, Brandon Suyeoka, Stanti Schönbächler, Brandy LaMotte, photographer Masano Kawana, and food stylist Toshiko Kawana.

If I've left anyone out, I apologize for the omission.

For those of you who knew my mother, I hope you can relive some of the wonderful memories we all shared cooking, eating and laughing together as you flip through this book.

Much love and Happy Cooking!

Published by Tuttle Publishing, an imprint of Periplus Editions (HK) Ltd.

www.tuttlepublishing.com

Library of Congress Cataloging-in-Publication Data

Chin, Katie.
  Katie Chin's everyday Chinese cookbook :
  101 delicious recipes from my mother's
  kitchen / Katie Chin.
      pages cm
  Includes index.
  ISBN 978-0-8048-4522-9 (hardcover)
  1. Cooking, Chinese. I. Title. II. Title: Everyday Chinese cooking.
  TX724.5.C5C56114 2016
  641.5951--dc23

                                                         2015017810

  ISBN: 978-0-8048-4522-9

DISTRIBUTED BY   *Asia Pacific*
North America, Latin America &   Berkeley Books Pte. Ltd.
Europe   61 Tai Seng Avenue #02-12
Tuttle Publishing   Singapore 534167
364 Innovation Drive   Tel: (65) 6280-1330
North Clarendon,   Fax: (65) 6280-6290
VT 05759-9436 U.S.A.   inquiries@periplus.com.sg
Tel: (802) 773-8930   www.periplus.com
Fax: (802) 773-6993
info@tuttlepublishing.com   20 19 18 17 16
www.tuttlepublishing.com   5 4 3 2 1
                                   Printed in Singapore   1511CP
Japan
Tuttle Publishing
Yaekari Building, 3rd Floor
5-4-12 Osaki, Shinagawa-ku
Tokyo 141 0032
Tel: (81) 3 5437-0171
Fax: (81) 3 5437-0755
sales@tuttle.co.jp
www.tuttle.co.jp

TUTTLE PUBLISHING® is a registered trademark of Tuttle Publishing, a division of Periplus Editions (HK) Ltd.

About Tuttle: "Books to Span the East and West"

Our core mission at Tuttle Publishing is to create books which bring people together one page at a time. Tuttle was founded in 1832 in the small New England town of Rutland, Vermont (USA). Our fundamental values remain as strong today as they were then—to publish best-in-class books informing the English-speaking world about the countries and peoples of Asia. The world has become a smaller place today and Asia's economic, cultural and political influence has expanded, yet the need for meaningful dialogue and information about this diverse region has never been greater. Since 1948, Tuttle has been a leader in publishing books on the cultures, arts, cuisines, languages and literatures of Asia. Our authors and photographers have won numerous awards and Tuttle has published thousands of books on subjects ranging from martial arts to paper crafts. We welcome you to explore the wealth of information available on Asia at **www.tuttlepublishing.com**.